LOVE HATE

BROOKS GIBBS

D1563139

LIFE STRATEGY SERIES

LOVE > HATE
The Ultimate Strategy to End Bullying
By Brooks Gibbs

Copyright © 2010 by Brooks Gibbs

Cover Photography by Christian Rios
Cover Design by AE Creative
Content Consulting and Development by Todd Hillard

Published in USA by BG Communications
Printed in USA by Lightning Source

Library of Congress Cataloging-in-Publication Data is available.

Gibbs, Brooks, 2010
[Love is Greater than Hate: The Ultimate Strategy to End Bullying]
Young Adults/Self-Help/Student Leadership

ISBN 978-0-615-35570-2

Manufactured in the United States of America

10 9 8 7 6 5 4 3 2 1

DEDICATION

To my two boys, Bradon and Jackson—the JOYS of my life. May your heart be full of compassion for the needs of others, and may you have the wisdom and resources to meet those needs.

ACKNOWLEDGMENTS

This book was inspired by my friend and mentor Gresham Hill. He has his pulse on youth culture, and really encouraged me to write a book addressing the growing bullying and cyber-bullying trends. I am grateful for his years of friendship and connecting me to Todd Hillard. Todd took my messy transcript and turned it into a clear message. I am a speaker, and don't consider myself a writer. Todd really encouraged me and had a profound influence on the finished product. He also connected me with a great young editor, Taylor Francis, who not only did a great job on edits but opened up her heart and provided valuable feedback on my solution to hate.

After all of our writing was done, Aric Everson, my life long graphics designer and creative consultant made this book visually appealing. He did a great job managing the cover and interior layout and I am most grateful for his patience with me—a novice writer.

I also want to acknowledge the incredible support and friendship of Ken and Deana Jones, who have encouraged and empowered me over the years to reach more youth.

Finally, I could not have done this book without the support of my wife, Jill. She has always supported my projects, re-arranging her whole life and daily schedule around the demands of my work. She is a true example of selfless love. I couldn't ask for a better life partner.

FOREWORD

I was a student at Columbine High School, home of the worst school shooting in America's history. I was sitting in the school library that day, which was the scene of the most intense shooting. There were 10 students that were killed around me and nearly 20 that were wounded. I saw two of my close friends killed right before my eyes. Later that same day I found out that my sister, Rachel Joy Scott, had also been killed.

Since that horrible event, my family and I have traveled to share Rachel's story in schools across the country. Rachel was a girl who would step out of her way in compassion to show kindness for other students that nobody else thought were important, or had value. She would stick up for students that were getting put down or picked on. She would sit by the kid that sat all alone at lunch. She reached out to a student that had a mental and physical disability who was having some thoughts of suicide, and she saved his life by just talking to him for a couple of minutes every day, giving him a hug, asking him how he was doing.

When we share this story, we give students like you a challenge to be a part of the chain reaction of love that my sister started. We've seen thousands of students accept this challenge. We're seeing a huge impact because students are able to look at Rachel as a role model—just a simple teenager that made a big difference because of what she believed in. Rachel was a person of value. She was a person of character, and she was a person of faith. She was killed for all of those things that day, but her legacy still lives on in the hearts of many students.

Brooks and I have been friends for a long time. After the Columbine shooting, we both dedicated our lives to combat the hate we see in schools with a message of love. As a result, we have met a lot of teens across this country that struggle with depression, loneliness, and anger—solid proof that this love message is needed. We both believe that by communicating messages that address the needs of the heart we will provide real value and substance instead of attempting to provide band-aid answers. It's a privilege to be able to do this and connect with the students on the deepest level possible.

I believe that the message of this book, *LOVE > HATE*, is truly the ultimate strategy to end bullying. Love, shown through kindness and compassion, is the best antidote to hate.

While school administrators everywhere try to focus on security measures to prevent the next tragedy, let's not forget that the best form of prevention is character education. Getting to the heart of the young students is what will change this growing trend of hate. We need to focus on setting parameters around our heart.

My dad, who is a scholar in American history, teaches that for the first 200 years of our education system, schooling focused on character first, then knowledge, and then academic achievement. However, in the last 50 years, character development has lost its top priority in schools. I think that incorporating character development back into our educational system is something that this generation is desperately crying out for. That is the reason why Brooks and I are challenging students like you to deal with the deeper issues of the heart. Develop your character.

So please, from the bottom of my heart, take this book seriously. Allow Brooks to ask you tough questions that may, at times, feel uncomfortable. We all need to do a heart check, and search for any hate that is poisoning our relationships. Brooks can help you with this. I hope you will take his challenge to live a life of LOVE, because it is our only hope.

Craig Scott
School Shooting Survivor

CONTENTS

WELCOME TO MY JUNGLE

I walked through the giant double doors of my new school and entered a huge lobby filled with students rushing to and from classes. I was overwhelmed at the site of so many young adults. I was just in 8th grade a few months before—feeling like the big man on campus at my middle school. But I was a tiny fish in a big pond now—a freshman on his first day in high school. Everyone was taller than me and seemed way more confident. I was scared to death.

Suddenly, a sharp pain ripped through my left shoulder and I spun to the ground. *Is this a heart attack? Anxiety attack? What is going on?* I rolled over and saw a towering giant hovering above me. He was a six-foot-something football player with fire in his eyes and his fist still clenched.

"No one stands on the buffalo!" he bellowed. "I said **no one** stands on the buffalo. Move!" I looked down and realized that I had been standing on a mosaic tile picture of a buffalo grazing on the prairie. Apparently this was our school's mascot, and a senior in high school was in the process of teaching me one of the unwritten rules of life beyond my middle school: If you disrespect the buffalo, you will pay.

I quickly stepped off the tile, only to discover that he wasn't done with me yet. He grabbed my shirt and pulled out a toothbrush before spitting on the mosaic. "Clean it!" (Wait. Isn't it more disrespectful to spit on something rather than accidently stand on it?!) Clearly something else was going on. This really wasn't about the buffalo. This was about anger, intimidation, fear and power. As hundreds of students cheered and laughed, I got down on my hands and knees and cleaned the tile. The blood rushed to my face, and I dropped my eyes in embarrassment. I thought to myself, *No way! Not this place too! I thought bullying was just a middle school thing. Weren't high school kids way more mature than this?*

Welcome to the World of Bullies. Bullies are everywhere. Just look around your school and you will see bullying all around you. Not just the typical big guy beating up the little guy stuff. Bullying is much broader than that stereotype. You can see it happen in the hallways between classes. Shoulders brush up against each other and cuss words are exchanged. In the bathrooms, a girl makes a snob comment about another girl's hair. In the cafeteria line, during check-out a student makes fun of another student for being poor—having to use the discount meal program—you know, the "Free and Reduced" lunch card that marks you as a target.

In the parking lot, one student parks her beat-up pickup truck next to a gloating girl's new Mustang. On the football field, a wide receiver misses a catch during practice and gets harassed by the quarterback. These hate moments are peppered throughout the school experience every day.

Bullying isn't what it used to be. The football player stealing the water-boy's milk money is the least of our worries these days. The stakes are higher now. When teens go to school, they are often going into a verbal war zone. The angry words of the bully are becoming more venomous. It's been years since the "you're a stupid head" phrase of kindergarten has been used. When people smack-talk each other at school, it transforms a safe learning environment into a hostile war zone. This is a lose/lose situation for everybody. School is hard enough trying to find good friends, keeping your grades up, and not burning out with all the clubs, sports, and events that you are encouraged to do.

The bullies are also taking the dirty smack-talking off campus and onto the internet. Ordinary students who have never bullied anyone are getting caught up in *cyber-bullying*, causing serious damage to their enemy. They send anonymous hate e-mail. They launch fake profiles on popular social network sites for the whole school to see. They even post embarrassing photos and make comments about them. As a result, the hurt is deeper now than ever. Life is hard enough to try and cope with your changing body, keeping peace with your family, and doing your best to feel good about yourself. When you throw bullying into the mix, life gets a million times more complicated.

Bullying is no joke. It really hurts people. With the increase in hate comes an increase in hurt. Today's victims of bullying are more depressed. They are at high risk for violence against their enemy, anxiety, depression, self-injurious behavior, and/or suicide.

Many teens wrongly believe that bullying is a necessary evil in their school. They feel that everyone says and does hurtful things to each other all of the time, and that there is no way to change it. Others think that there is ultimately no real problem with bullying and that even if there was something wrong, nothing can be done about it anyway.

To that I say "NO WAY!" and I hope that this book proves that flawed thinking to be wrong.

That first morning at my new high school was absolutely horrible. I felt degraded. I felt embarrassed. I felt powerless. Finally, the bully let me go and I tried to disappear into the crowd. Was I going to have to hide forever? Then I started to do some thinking. It was obvious that if I didn't do something about bullying in my school, I would have four years of hell in front of me. That was not an option. I thought, *I must make this school a happier place. I don't want anyone to be humiliated like I have been.* That's when a dream was born in my heart—a dream to make my school a better place.

I soon found out that I wasn't alone. With over 150 days spent in school each year, little bits of hate can really burden a student. Just ask around and you will find that students are fed up with the negativity and wish that school could be a more positive experience. I discovered that right away and soon we started to make a difference together. I am proud to say that through four years of focused effort, my dream came true. I changed my school for the better.

In this book I'm going to be brutally honest with you, giving you full access to my heart—and it's not all pretty. You see, I've been on *both* sides of the bully/victim conflict. But this book is ultimately not about me—it is really about YOU. I want to help you understand just how bad the bully problem is in this country. I want to show you what's really at the heart of the bully problem. (Hatred: caused by hurt, prejudices, and intolerance.) Then I want to see you catch a vision to be a part of the solution. (Love: shown through respect, kindness, and compassion.) I believe that love is the antidote for hatred. Genuine love is what has always worked in times passed, and is what is working wonders for schools today. Simply put, love conquers all. In the pages ahead, you're going to get it all about bullying: the *concern*, the *cause*, the *cure*, and the *change strategy* that can transform you and your school for the better.

You can also be sure that I will be giving you proven strategies for you and your friends to use to end bullying on your campus. Get your pen out and get ready to do some serious reflection because I will be asking you some important questions too. If you are going to be a part of the extreme change that we so desperately need in this country, I need you to be committed.

So before we start, I want you to sign the promise paragraph below. By signing this, you are committing to work through this book honestly and completely. Loads of energy and research have been put into the pages you now hold in your hand... all I am asking in return is total dedication to complete this book from cover to cover. I am proud of you for taking this challenge! So sign it. Seriously—you need to do this...so go on!

"I promise to work through this book honestly and openly so that I might be a part of the change that we need in our generation. I believe that bullying is hurtful and wrong, and I am committed to help stop it."

Signed: _____   Date: _____

Excellent! Let's dig in right away. The sooner we work together, the sooner bullying will stop! Now, turn the page...

Let me flip things around a bit. This may seem like a bad time to be in school, but I actually think that it is the best time for you, and I am not being overly optimistic either. Extreme times call for extreme measures, and I believe that there is an extreme answer to this devastating trend of bullying. We don't need stricter policies (although I think every school should have solid policies against bullying. The "no weapons" rule is always a good idea.) The answer is not *more* police, teacher, or parental presence on campus. (Yes, I said parental. Can you imagine your mom as the hall monitor? Lovely.)

The answer to this bullying epidemic is... Brace Yo'Self... I'm about to say it... Wait for it... It's YOU, the student! *(Imagine inspiring battle drums, as you read the rest of this paragraph.)* The end of bullying begins with you. You are the only hope we have to end bullying on campus and online, because you make decisions every day to either hurt others by your negative words and actions, or you help them by your genuine kindness and compassion.

You can join the growing movement of young people who are taking matters into their own hands by starting a domino effect of love—changing every student in the school for the better.

You really can. Trust me. I've been there...on both sides.

THE CONCERN:
THE BIG BULLYING PICTURE...
AND SOME LITTLE DETAILS

I'll never forget Amanda. I met her when she came to our high school as a new girl that had moved into the area. At first no one cared much about her. She sort of just blended in with the rest of the students. She didn't talk much and never drew attention to herself. By the end of the school year, however, she was the most hated girl in school. She was tormented by other girls, and I honestly don't remember anyone standing up for her. People at my school fostered a growing hatred towards her. It was a slow progression of verbal abuse that was one of the saddest things I had ever seen. There was no doubt something was awkward about her—she was one of those types who could never be cool even if she tried. Her clothes were mismatched, her hair frizzy and without style. Even her backpack and locker were disheveled with papers and books. It didn't help that she was overweight either. At the end of the year, she told me that she was considering dropping out. The mean girls that attacked her daily were making her life unbearable.

Amanda was a target for hate, and it seemed to be getting worse by the day. She was hoping that her parents would eventually move out of the area so she could transfer schools. I knew deep down inside that no matter where she would go, she would be a target for mean bullies. Something about her personality just drew it out of other students. Don't get me wrong, she was a nice girl—just awkward, uncoordinated and uncool. For these things, which she could not control, they were slowly torturing her.

Amanda was the one who showed me that bullying was not just a physical attack from someone bigger and stronger. She taught me that bullying is mostly a verbal attack. Words are the primary tool that bullies use to intimidate and harass their victims. In Amanda's case, physical fights were not her problem. Hateful words from other girls were the thing that she had to endure. And she's not alone; this is an issue that has reached epidemic proportions on campuses and online. It is damaging the emotional psyche of students your age everywhere. Check this out: 160,000 students skip school everyday in America to avoid being bullied. For those that are brave enough to go to school, 6 out of 10 of them witness bullying at least once a day.[1] Needless to say, this is a real problem and we (including you) have to do something to stop it.

1.1 Bullying Can Be:

Physical: This one's easy to recognize. Examples include pushing, shoving, hitting, kicking, biting, hair-pulling, inappropriate touch, breaking objects, and taking or damaging another person's stuff.

Verbal: It's really common because it's quick, direct, and easy to do. Examples include teasing, name-calling, threats, intimidation, demeaning jokes, rumors, gossip, and slander.

Emotional: This type of bullying is more sophisticated. It's calculated and often done by a group. Nasty stuff. It hurts people on the inside and makes them feel bad about themselves. Examples include leaving someone out on purpose, telling lies to hurt someone's reputation, and humiliating someone publicly.

Cyber-bullying: Using technology is the newest way to bully. Examples include sending mean text messages, posting videos, stories, or photos that ridicule someone, and spreading rumors through social networking sites.

Here are some real emails from teens reporting bully scenarios they are in the middle of:

Allie writes:

There's this kid who is getting pushed around and teased a lot. He dresses kind of different and acts weird sometimes. When kids tease him, he gets real mad. I'm scared to do anything, but he doesn't deserve this. He has no friends and seems really sad.

Cassie writes:

The good news: I scored a new cell phone with 1,000 texts per month for my birthday! The bad news: After about a week of texting my friends, my BFF started sending messages like "no one likes U" and "every1 hates being bothered by your stupid texts." Some friend! I don't want to tell my parents because they might take my phone away.

Alex writes:

My best friend was at a party last weekend. Kids were drinking beer and vodka, and some were getting really crazy. Like one girl was dancing, then she took off her top and kept on dancing. It was just for a minute, but my friend took some pictures with his camera phone. He showed them to me at school today and said he was going to send them to the entire class. I think that is so uncool, but the dude is my friend.

T.J. writes:

I'm new at my school, and making friends is really hard. Most of the kids here have known each other since they were in kindergarten. I just don't fit in. They don't even give me a chance. They make fun of the way I talk and dress, and they all laugh at me. At my last school, I didn't have a lot of friends, but the ones I had were great. Going to school totally sucks. I make excuses to stay home as often as I can.

Jack writes:

There's this guy at school who likes making me mad. He says stuff to me, then laughs when I get angry. My dad just says to just ignore him, but I get so mad I can't. So yesterday I took a swing at the kid. We both ended up in the office; I got suspended, and he only got detention. It's so not fair! He's doing this to me, and I'm the one who gets punished.

Kaylie writes:

We have a bus stop bully who's picking on littler kids—stealing their hats and filling them with snow, and stuff like that. Everyone is scared of him. We all think it will get worse if we say anything. Help!

Laura writes:

Do kids who call other people "retard" and "gay" even know what they're saying? My brother has Down syndrome, and it really hurts me when people use a word that makes fun of who he is. Same with "gay." It's used to insult everything unpopular—"your shirt is so gay!"—so it's like saying kids who are gay are rejects. Everybody just laughs and goes along when they hear it.

Taylor writes:

Personally, I have engaged in bullying activites and not realized it at the time, only to recognize what had been done almost a year later. I felt bad at the time, but I didn't outright KNOW that it was bullying. I just wanted to stop joining in with the rest of my group and ignore the situation. I think that a lot of teens are also oblivious to the fact that some of the things going on around them are considered bullying, but they are.

1.2 BULLYING IN THE MEDIA

Watching my friend Amanda being bullied by mean girls opened my eyes to the incredible hatred that filled the hearts of students in our school. I couldn't believe how girls could treat someone with such incredible disrespect. Just because she was different, they expressed their low opinion of her to her face and behind her back on a daily basis.

So, where does all of this hatred in schools come from? Why is everyone so mean? Well, I believe that bullying is a learned behavior. Bullies either see it at home, or they see it in the world around them. And let me tell you, there is a boatload of hate in our world today. The news media openly trashes other people, every day, all day. If you open your eyes, you will see it almost every time you catch the news.

We live in a blood-thirsty culture that thrives on juicy bits of gossip and slander. Our news outlets have become tabloid platforms that seek to exploit people and stir up the anger of the public. Our news commentators have become master bullies—not necessarily because they have been hurt by someone, but because bullying has become the popular thing to do. Hatred is BIG business. Why? Because of ratings! The more shocking and controversial the story, the more it peaks the public interest and people everywhere are more eager to watch—which in turn brings in more advertising dollars for networks. This downward spiral of sensationalizing hate has successfully fanned the flames of hatred in our world. We are at risk of becoming increasingly intolerant and hostile towards others who don't share our ideals.

In this dog-eat-dog world, anger has become a "virtue." Even our "role model" politicians run campaign ads that slander their competition's character. Turn on 24-hour cable news or talk radio, and you discover talking hot-heads propped up on their soap box, dishing out their hostile opinions without apology. Everyone seems to be screaming out their own agenda and pointing fingers. They relate to each other through turbo-charged suspicion, shotgun blasts of opinion and open hatred.

Very clearly, we have entered a new era. In this news media driven, "Information Age," issues like immigration, the war on terror, global warming, abortion, homosexuality, school violence, and gun control can only be discussed in anger. The old-fashioned form of polite discussion of the issues of the day has deteriorated into a shouting match. No wonder students in your school are so quick to be mean and hateful. Hatred is all around you.

1.3 THE UNSATISFIED APPETITE OF HATE

Hate grows if you feed it. I saw this firsthand as I watched the girls at school foster their hatred for Amanda. Every month the unfolding drama worsened and Amanda's countenance reflected her pain. Over time, she lost any happiness that she had once possessed. Through my observations, I have discovered that hate fully develops in three stages. Starting as a seemingly innocent judgmental prejudice, it grows into unfair discrimination before finally flaming into targeted violence.

1. Prejudice. Being prejudiced is simply holding a negative opinion of someone based on his or her personality, sexuality, race, gender, or appearance. When you think poorly of someone, you are inviting hatred into your mind. For Amanda, this happened on her first day of school. When she went to her first class, people observed her and started to hold a negative opinion of her. It was easy to think that she was poor, stupid, and nerdy. Any student who just looked at the way she dressed, and listened to her when she talked could identify that she was awkward. Because of this outward appearance, all of us at school laughed at her inside our minds. This is a sad example of having a prejudice. All of us, especially the mean girls, jumped to conclusions about her—before we even had a chance to get to know her.

If I know anything about the brain, I know that it loves to judge people and hold opinions about them. If you start viewing someone in a negative light, your brain will work hard to continue building a case against this person—adding up faults and negative information. You will soon only be able to see them in one way.

It may not seem like a bad thing to have negative opinions of others, but I firmly believe it is wrong. Shallow people judge a person's worth by the outside. Caring people seek to have deep conversations to get to know them on the inside. Even if it is popular to be prejudiced against someone, the right thing to do is to make an extra effort to think highly of that person so that you don't fall into the same trap as all the others have. If you hang out with prejudiced people, you are tempting your mind with hate food. It won't take long for you to hold the same negative opinions of others on your own.

2. Discrimination. Discrimination is simply treating others unfairly based on your judgmental prejudices. It is your judgments acted out. This is one of the most hurtful ways to hate someone. It's bad enough to judge a person, but it takes hate to a whole new level when you start treating them differently based on your negative judgments. I saw this happen almost immediately with Amanda. At lunch time, she would always go straight for the table in the corner of the cafeteria to sit alone. It was as if she knew that no one would accept her. No one did accept her. The whole year that she was at our school, I don't ever remember her having a close friend. Loneliness is one of the worse feelings in the world. The other girls were definitely guilty of discrimination. They took the prejudiced thoughts that were in their mind and acted on them by rejecting her in public.

Rejection is painful; when you push someone out of your "cool group" because they failed to be as cool as you, you are discriminating against them. Whenever you alienate someone, you are humiliating them in front of others. We should never try and determine who is worthy of our attention and who is not.

You can't treat people like you treat clothing. If you don't like a certain type of shirt, you have the option to just cast it away, but you can't do that to a person. People have feelings, and one of the strongest needs we all have is to belong and be accepted.

3. Assault. The final stage of hate will show itself through assault. This is when you physically or emotionally attack another person in order to inflict pain on them. You can't get more evil than targeted assault. This can start with name calling and lead to injury depending on your temperament. Bottom line: Starting a fight with someone using your fists, weapons, or even your words is never okay.

Amanda was a victim of verbal assault. I remember one time when she showed me a folded up piece of paper that someone had given her. I opened it up and saw a disturbing drawing that was supposed to look like her. The drawing was of Amanda's face covered in zits. There was a caption that read: *"Drrrrr... I'm a retard.... I have no friends.... I suck as a human... Drrrrr.... I just pissed my pants..."* Then at the bottom of the picture were the words, *"Do us all a favor and leave, go away, or die."*

Needless to say, Amanda was weeping. This hate-note cut her deeply. I remember just putting my arm around her and apologizing for all of the attacks that she had to endure. My heart broke for her, and I was deeply angry that these ruthless attacks were from fellow students.

A person who assaults another person hoping to inflict physical or emotional pain is profoundly immature, and has a deep need to overpower their victim to feel better about themselves. It may be revenge that they are looking for, or maybe just the sick satisfaction of making someone cry—if you ever get to this level, you have allowed hate to hijack your life. You are no longer in control. Your hate has overpowered your conscience. Hatred is dictating your every move, and like a strategist in battle, your mind is working around the clock to find ways to inflict more and more pain.

Amanda told me that day that she wanted to kill those girls. I was in shock, because I could tell that she was being serious. They pushed her to her limit; she could only endure so much abuse. It had finally pushed her over the edge. I promised her that I would try and stop these girls from their vicious attacks. I could see in her eyes that she was deeply wounded, more than ready to inflict pain on her enemies. It scared me, for her sake.

I walked with Amanda to the guidance counselor's office and helped her fill out a detailed report of the harassment she endured everyday at school. We made a copy of the hate-note that she had just received in the hopes that the counselor would see the seriousness of the situation. I was so proud of Amanda; she had finally confessed her anger to the counselor. She said that she had considered taking her own life or the lives of the mean girls. This alarmed the counselor, who then committed herself to protect Amanda from ever being humiliated like that again.

To be honest with you, I think that if our counselor didn't help Amanda, she would have killed herself. She might have even killed her enemies. Amanda was a good person that never deserved the bullying that she received; but the constant attacks from those mean girls had the potential to make her into a murderer.

Don't think for a second that you are too good of a person to ever allow yourself to stoop so low. Anyone can become so affected by bullying that they respond in violence. Violent bullying produces violent victims. If we, like Amanda, allow our mind to grow in hatred toward our enemies, we will end up fighting back and hurting them. It's just a matter of time.

1.4 MY STORY

Growing up, I struggled with self-worth. The negative words that my peers would say to me really hurt. I didn't feel valuable at all. I hated the way I looked. I hated that I was shorter than everyone in my class and the bullies constantly reminded me by calling me names—like "shorty," "shrimp," "midget," etc. I remember trying to stretch my back to make myself taller. I even tried to stuff cardboard in the heels of my shoes to try and gain an inch or two. I wasn't athletic by any stretch of the imagination. I had severe asthma and was dependent on an inhaler to get through sports games. It wouldn't have surprised me if I had an asthma attack playing Nintendo. You should have seen me—even the way I walked was so wimpy. My chest caved in a bit, my frame was frail and sickly, and it didn't take much to make me cry.

I was pretty much a failure in school and struggled to make decent grades. I was unsure of myself, and my speech impediment proved it. I spent many years in special education programs in hopes that the extra dedicated teachers would bring me up to speed with the rest of my classmates. I'm not a psychologist, but I imagine my stuttering problem could have been triggered by my lack of confidence to speak what was on my mind. I was incredibly intimidated by others; I have numerous memories of not being able to look at people in the eyes. If I did, I could feel my face get flushed and I would well up with tears for no reason at all. I would have to look away, and the person I would be talking with would be terribly confused. Needless to say, I became a perfect target for a bully.

One of the biggest bullies in our elementary school was named "Snortin' Norton." He got his name from a bad habit that he had of snorting white-out and other toxic paint products to get high. I never actually knew his first name. I really hated him though. This guy would always try and intimidate me. If I ever came close to him he would cuss me out and threaten to punch me. I'll never forget one day after school, when Snortin' Norton came out from under a ditch where he was hiding, waiting for me as I was walking home. My heart leaped out of my chest. I ran as hard as I could, unable to stay ahead of him. He grabbed me by my backpack and started to punch my chest as hard as he could. I asked him why he was being so mean, and he just repeatedly told me that he hated me. I went home bruised and in shock. I just couldn't understand what I had ever done to deserve such abuse from someone.

In middle school there was another kid that we called "Stuff" (who got his name from his ability to play basketball.) He cornered me in the locker room and gave me a painful "titty-twister" (Pinching my nipple as hard as he could). He wouldn't let go until I yelled "I'm a girl" or something like that. I was crying in pain, telling him to stop but he refused. He was incredibly strong with a mean temper. After letting go of me he shoved me out of his way and pounded his fist in the middle of my back as hard as he could. I fell to the ground with the wind knocked out of me. My chest was bleeding and I was sure that he broke my back with his fist. The other students just stood around and laughed. Once again, I had nothing against this kid. I never provoked him to fight me. He just decided that I was someone he wanted to bully. I felt like there was no justice. No teachers intervened. No students stood up for me. I was left alone to scrape together my shattered dignity after this painful humiliation.

You would think that my horrible experience of being bullied and hurt by others would make me more compassionate towards other loser students like me. I am sorry to say that I was anything but compassionate. I was a part of the negative domino effect of all of my insecurities and hurt. Occasionally, another kid would show up who was actually lower than me in the un-coolness department (out of the 1.5 billion teens on the planet, about 8 fell in this category). The bullies would then shift their focus off of me and onto this poor guy. Whenever this window of opportunity would appear, I considered it my chance to prove myself as an equal to the "popular" kids.

I remember a kid that wore his Boy Scout uniform to school every Wednesday. We all thought he looked really stupid in that outfit, and I joined up with the other bullies, trying my best to say the most hurtful things I could come up with. This won me some points as a "cool" kid, but every time I treated someone else like scum, I felt so much shame inside. I knew how much it hurt to be laughed at, yelled at, threatened, and teased. I began to hate myself even more for being so mean to them. I knew it was wrong, but for some reason I just kept on doing it. I would bully others whenever the bullies would take their eyes off of me.

Despite the shame I felt inside, I continued down this path of anger. In time, I became a completely different person. In middle school, I joined a local gang in my neighborhood called the "Street Angels." (Scary, huh? Imagine Malcolm in the Middle, trying to turn into a Mexican gangster, drinking cervezas and smoking doobies with the homeboys.) Our crew ran around nearby neighborhoods and swiped hood ornaments off of nice cars. We smashed windows with rocks. We stole stuff from little kids and made them wet their pants in horror. We got drunk and high and did things I don't even remember. At my lowest point, I was actually arrested for attacking a car with a hammer. What was I thinking? I guess you could say that I wasn't thinking. I was just following the Street Angels...and I was unhappier than I had ever been before. I hated the hate.

Listen, if you had known me back then, you would've been convinced that I was a first-class jerk, because that's how I was acting. I take full responsibility for my actions and my attitudes, but I also know that no one is born a bully. Bullies are made over time by the people who hurt them. When we were born we were absolute clean slates—until hurt penetrated the heart. Seeds of hurt start to grow inside every time we are let down by others—especially those closest to us. If we don't get control of it, we become pathetic little wanna-be thugs...at least that's what most people saw when they looked at me.

You know what I'm talking about. Let's be honest. Because all of us hurt, we in turn hurt others. I believe that we are all bullies at some level. We all show signs that there is hatred inside of us. If we don't help the bully within us, than we won't be able to help the bullies around us. Let me ask you a few difficult questions. You must answer honestly.

1. Do you ever call other people names? (Friends, brothers/sisters, teachers, parents, etc.)

2. Do you laugh when someone makes a mistake? (When someone drops their pecan pie in the lunch room, or when someone slips and falls on their rear in the locker room. How about when an embarrassing picture circulates around the Internet.)

3. Do you laugh or refuse to intervene when someone is being bullied right in front of you? (When the tall jock holds the short kid's backpack too high in the air for him to reach, or when a teacher makes a fellow student feel stupid for asking a dumb question.)

4. Do you refuse to help someone when they need it? (Help with a math equation, help with a ride home, help with a project, help meet new friends, help your family, etc.)

5. Do you enjoying seeing your enemies suffer? (Fail a test, get cut from the team, get injured, get caught for wrongdoing, etc.)

6. Do you feel hate towards anyone in your heart/mind? (Maybe an over-dramatic peer, mean bully, annoying sibling, harsh teachers, strict parents, controlling boss, etc.)

7. Do you avoid interacting with some people that you don't care for? (People who are different than you, those who are in a different grade, or have a disability, etc.)

8. Do you stereotype/label people? (Based on social status, religious beliefs, popularity, or the color of their skin? Maybe you label them by the type of clothes they wear, whether they are good looking or ugly, fat or skinny, smart or dumb, skaters, jocks, nerds/geeks, blondes, sluts, Gothic, etc.)

9. Do you think you are better than other people? (Better looking, smarter, cooler, more talented, richer, etc.)

10. Do you get other people (including friends) in trouble? (Get them to smoke, do drugs, have sex, cheat on tests, start fights, skip school, miss curfew, etc.)

11. Do you have bad thoughts towards anyone? (Annoyed by them, think they are dumb, etc.)

12. Do you ever blow up at your parents, or fight with them disrespectfully?

13. Do you ever call your brother or sister names, physically hurt them, or yell at them?

If you answered "yes" to any of these questions, then welcome to the club. You are a bully. You—yes, you—are a bully. A bully is *anyone* who subtracts value from another person by their words or actions. A friend of mine taught me that every interaction in life is mathematical.

Every time you interact with someone you can add or subtract with your words. What you say can breathe fresh life into someone, add to them. Or, what you say can suck the life out of someone, subtract from them. Basically, there are at least two ways to say everything: nice and not nice.[2] When you are mean to others, you steal from them. You take away their dignity, happiness, and sense of belonging, and you degrade yourself in the process.

Oh how I wish every student would realize that we all have back-stories of hurt and pain caused by things outside of school. I wish that we would treat each other with proper respect, knowing that life is hard enough growing up. We don't need fighting, gossiping, cursing, backbiting, spreading rumors, etc. Those things make life so much harder. School should be a place of understanding, encouragement, and bettering ourselves. Sadly though, it is not.

Hurt people hurting people. That's the cycle.

There is a domino effect that happens at every school—everywhere. The negative hate that is dished out through words and actions, brings out more negative hate. Bullying creates more bullying, which creates more bullying. And on and on it goes.

1.5 Sooooo, WHAT Now?

OK, let's recap: we've got the concern. We understand the rampant problem with bullying, and we're motivated to do something about it. We also understand the *cause*. People who have been hurt will hurt others, causing a domino effect that multiplies again and again. But where do we start to make a change?

School administrators have come up with some nifty ideas. It seems to me that they either ignore the issue and do nothing (crossing their fingers, hoping nothing really bad happens) or they go to the other extreme and punish anything that remotely looks like bullying.

- A kid in Palm Beach, Florida was charged with "using an egg as a deadly weapon."

- In New Jersey, two students were accused of "Terrorism: playing cops and robbers with a paper gun."[3]

- A school I recently spoke at in Orange City, Iowa had signs on campus that said,
  "No Tolerance for Bullying, No Way, Never! Or Else..."

These schools that go extreme call it a "Zero Tolerance" policy, but the students tell me that they feel like they are being bullied by the teachers not to bully. *Oops, counterproductive.* While I am a HUGE fan of schools adopting policies that prevent bullying, sometimes the extreme policies have an adverse affect. Don't you think? For example, in this "zero tolerance" school in Iowa, they severely punished even the pettiest arguments in the hallways. This in turn caused a lot of students to **not** report any bullying incidents for fear of receiving a punishment that didn't fit the crime.

Lectures by administrators and teachers sometimes only fuel the fire. Unless students have a high level of respect, administrators can have the opposite effect and the behavior goes through the roof. One girl said she had a teacher in the 6th grade who told a boy to stop saying "gay," and when the student replied with, "That is so homosexual," the teacher gave him a referral. Even though the boy was punished, the incident ended up becoming a joke amongst her class. No one took the teacher seriously.

In Orange City, the school also cracked down on "hate speech" that offended or was discriminatory in any way. So T-shirts with an upside down cross were confiscated and the person who said something like "your mom goes to college," was immediately expelled. This caused many students feel like they were actually being stripped of their First Amendment right—Freedom of Speech and Expression. Carefully worded laws regarding "hate speech" might be a step in the right direction, and might help eliminate insulting non-truths, but other laws could destroy the ability to point out the true, concrete wrong in others.

I have seen the bullying worsen over the last 10 years that I have been speaking to students *and* I am seeing a growing frustration between students and faculty, parents and principals. No one seems to know how to end this horrible, growing epidemic. But have no fear, the Bullyologist is here! (Brooks enters center stage with sparkly tights, flowy cape, chest sticking out with part smile and part "Grrrrrr!")

Here's the point: If we are going to find a *cure*, we must face the *cause*! Since life comes with its fair share of painful let downs, I actually believe that hurt resides in us all. If you are human, you have been hurt, and that hurt is deep down in you. How much is in you? Only you can be sure. Seeds of hurt will always grow into hate if you remain unhealed. You see, if you have been hurt by someone, and your hurt grows into hate for that person, you are on the fast track to bullying others. That is just the way it works. When you hate someone who has hurt you, you will unknowingly take it out on someone else. You will find a person to unleash all of your hate onto. This is your most basic coping mechanism.

There are two reasons why we bullies do what we do.

1. We fall into a trap of thinking it's just the cool thing to do, especially when our friends are doing it.

2. We have bottled up so much hurt inside of our hearts and minds, to the point that we must hurt other people to feel better about ourselves.

I know this is twisted, but it is the god-honest truth: *Hurting people hurt people in hopes that their pain will transfer to someone else.* We bullies will do whatever we have to do to make someone know that we disapprove of them. We ignore them, say bad things about them, do pranks, spread rumors, etc. Mostly we use our words. Our words are an unruly evil, full of deadly poison. We use our words to cause untold emotional damage to our victim, who then turns on someone else.

For a while it makes us feel powerful and in control. It may even make us feel better about ourselves. But these feelings only last for a short period of time. Then we have to do it again, and no amount of school policy or state laws can stop us.

Bullying is an issue of the heart. If we want to find the true cure for the bullying epidemic, that's where we need to start: *the heart.*

THE CURE:
THE END OF BULLYING
BEGINS WITH YOU

Bullying pushed me over the edge, and bullying sucked me in. There's really no other way to describe it. Yeah, I took my share of abuse, and then through stupid choices I turned around and dished it out to others. It was a horrible cycle. I felt like there was no way to get out.

But you know something? At night, when I would try and fall asleep, I would oftentimes reach that in-between space of wakefulness and dreams. At that moment I would remember the unconditional love that my mother would always show me. For a few minutes I would hear the kind words that the teachers would say to me. All of this would flood into my heart, and I was caught up in hope. For just a moment, I would believe them—and I could almost see myself as being a better person, someone who was making right choices, someone who was full of kindness to others. In my mind's eye, I spoke with confidence and courage. I had no enemies and I hurt no one. But then I would wake up and reality would always pull me out of that fantasy. The truth was that my whole life was falling in a downward spiral.

When I was in high school I finally realized why I was so stuck: I was miserable because of the anger and hatred I had inside. I never thought that life could get any better. I honestly just figured that I would live the rest of my life with a big chip on my shoulder. I decided that I was always going to live negatively towards the people around me. Thank God I was wrong.

I stumbled upon a healing process that changed my life forever. It was a key that unlocked all of my pain, resentment, anger, and hatred towards the people in my life that let me down—not just for a little while, but once and for all. Once I was able to learn this process to healing, I was able to address every hurt one by one, and systematically remove it from my life. I had found the cure to my misery and the cure to bullying of all kinds.

Let's face it: hate is toxic. It poisons your happiness. Hate will steal your youth. Hate is much like a weed. *It will grow like crazy and can only be killed when you pull it out by the root*—completely cast it away, root and all. That is why I fundamentally believe that **the end of bullying begins with you.** As Gandhi so eloquently said, "You must be the change that you want to see in this world."[4] If you want to change your school, you must change yourself. You are going to have to get to the root of any anger that you feel towards others. Maybe you're thinking, *but I don't hate anyone, and I don't think I am angry.* I would simply say to that, *you're wrong.* People let us down all of the time. People hurt us, and it has an effect on us.

Bullying is caused by deep-rooted hurt that has been experienced in the past, and all of us have wounds like these. The root of your anger could very well be the person that hurt you or bullied you when you were younger.

Is the situation hopeless? Are you trapped with no way of escape? It might feel like it, but that's not the truth. No, and I can say that for a fact. Because if you have made it this far in the book, I know something about you: *You want to live differently. You desire to not only be free from the hurt that bullies have caused you, but you want to be free from hurting others yourself.* This is called "above the line" living.

2.1 LIVING ABOVE THE LINE

One of the organizations I work very closely with is called the Pais Project[5] led by my good friend and mentor, Paul Gibbs (of no relation to me). Paul wrote a book called *The Cloud and the Line* where he beautifully illustrates how we should choose to live beyond right and wrong, reaching our highest ethical potential.

The line represents the standard of right and wrong. If you live *on* the line you believe that bullying is wrong, talking bad about others is wrong, and judging others is wrong. This is good, but not great—*it's not enough to change your life and those around you.*

If you live *below* the line, you are a common bully and have been hurt by others. You, in turn, hurt other people because it is portrayed as the "cool" thing to do, and you feel better about yourself. This is where the bullies dwell—by choice.

The cloud, however, represents a kind of life that is lived far *above* the norm. Going beyond right and wrong and reaching to the heights of extreme love. Most world changers lived on this level. If you choose to live in the clouds, you don't seek revenge when people hurt you. You don't speak badly of your enemies. You refuse to remain angry towards someone and always find ways to be healed from hurt, moving forward into a life that is at peace with everyone.

Most people aren't willing to live at this level, but I want to challenge you to rise above average and go for it. The line is crowded with good people. I want you to join me—and the others like me—as we strive to live beyond "good" and reach for what is best. It's time to seize our highest ethical potential and become radical world changers. This is the only way we will be able to see a profound change in our lives and on our campuses.

But in order to make that a reality, we have to add one more absolutely essential ingredient to the equation. This is the one key ingredient that allows you to mature to this level: *Love.*

2.2 THE LOVE STRATEGY

"Love" is probably the most misunderstood word in the world. Part of the problem is that we use this one word to describe many things. We water down its meaning by overuse. *I love my car. I love America. I love pizza. I love my computer. I love you. I would love to have my back rubbed.* We use the word *love* in so many different ways that it has literally lost its meaning. And how are we supposed to give or receive love when we don't even understand what it is? Dang, no wonder everything is so messed up! Let's see if we can straighten it up a bit:

LOVE ≠ FEELING

Most people think love is a feeling—a sentimental knot in the stomach, a quiver in the liver, an ocean of emotion. That one lie messes us up big time. Listen, it's true that love *can* produce feelings, but it is *more* than a feeling.

LOVE = CHOICE + ACTION

Most people also think that love is uncontrollable. Have you ever said, "I fell in love" as if you had tripped? We hear people say stuff like "I can't help it if I'm in love." Or the opposite: "I can't help myself; I just don't love him anymore." We talk as if love is uncontrollable, but that's a lie too. If you're going to live above the line there are two things you must believe about love:

- *Love is a choice.*

- *Love is an action.*

Get this: love *is* controllable. We have total control over whom we love and whom we don't love… and I believe that we should love all people. It's a choice we make.

Love is also something we do. It is an action. The Greeks had four words to differentiate the types of love: *storge,* which means natural affection; *eros,* which means sexual attraction; *philia,* which means emotional affection or friendship; and *agape,* which means unconditional, giving, sacrificial love.

This last type of love, *agape,* is the greatest form of love and has the power to turn enemies into friends. This type of love overlooks the bad in people and gives to them without wanting anything in return. Too often we love just with words and not with actions. Love is more than words and more than feelings. When you choose this kind of love, your pride will hate it. But something inside of you (your soul), knows that this type of love is what you need to give to others. If you want to live above the line of average, you must have agape love.

LOVE > HATE

The ones who hurt us need our love the most. In fact, I believe that this is the ultimate pathway to healing—to turn the hate that you feel towards someone into genuine love and care for them. I know that sounds totally nuts and backwards from everything we have been taught in the media, even going against some of our most basic instincts. But I actually believe, *and have experienced firsthand,* that it is possible to love those who have hurt you through this high level of love.

My sister was the one who is responsible for dragging me into a group of people who understood this kind of love. When all hell was cutting loose in my life, she talked me into going to her youth group where I saw something entirely different going on. There was an authentic genuine love that was spewing out of that group. Now, I know not all youth groups are that way, but this one was. I saw something that deep down inside I knew I wanted…and I knew this was the key to overcoming hate and bullying.

Get this: We often learn by example. I could read books on love, but when someone comes into my life who is a very loving person, I will have more of a chance of changing into a loving person by observing them than if I try to read about it or make it up. Yeah, this youth group showed me love and then they showed me where they believed it came from. For me, the ultimate truth is this: If we really want to know love, we need to discover how much God loves us. I believe that the more we discover how much he loves us, the more we will open up with more capacity to love our enemies. We learn by example, and for me, the greatest example of love has been my relationship with God—how he accepts me and forgives me—along with the teachings of Christ about how he came to this earth completely with one agenda: to love us. Now I find that the closer I get to him, the more I have the capacity to love others.

Please listen to me carefully: what I'm saying is that it is possible to love people who are seemingly "unlovable." It's possible to love even your "enemies." I'm not saying that it's *easy.* I'm saying it's *possible.* Sure, it is easy to love people who are kind and lovely, but love really shines when hard-to-love people come into our lives, and we choose to love them despite what they have done to us.

The truth is our lives are full of people we don't like. We do not like the way some people talk. We don't like the way some act and dress. But most of all, we tend not to like the people who do not like us. If you were to think about it for sixty seconds, you could probably come up with a list of people you do not like. They would probably be people whom you have trouble getting along with. I am not promoting the idea that you have to like everyone. (Isn't that a relief?) Some people are really mean and have little to like about them. But I do believe that you must show love towards everyone, even your enemies. When you are able to sincerely love those who are seemingly unlovable, your whole life changes.

Remember, love isn't a feeling. It's a choice and it's an action. Love does not necessarily mean that you have to have warm affections, feelings, or emotions towards them. *In fact, when you first choose to show them love, it will go against every feeling in your body.* You won't want to do it. But if you press on, your feelings will dramatically change towards that person.

Okay, I imagine that when you picked up this book, you didn't expect to do such personal soul searching, but I hope you are willing to trust me! If you follow my example and the example of other brave teens and adults, you will rise above your own hatred towards other people. You will be living above the line and experience a heart full to the brim with love for others... even your enemies.

So hang on tight here, because for this to be real, we have to get really personal. I need you to think about someone. Think really hard. Think about someone who has hurt you pretty good. If you don't know who has hurt you, you won't be able to experience the healing that I am talking about. So, think about the person that has hurt you the most—if that's too rough, maybe think about somebody who hasn't hurt you quite so bad. But I'm looking for someone who caused a lot of pain, and has negatively influenced your life.

Got'em? Good. Now...

Now I am going to ask you to choose to love that person. I know this seems impossible, but please believe me when I say that you need to show them unconditional, giving, and sacrificial love. No, they don't deserve your love, but you are going to show them love anyways, because you're living above the line, because you choose to turn your back on the built up hatred that you feel towards them, and you choose to be free.

To be honest with you, that painful person in my life was my dad. When I think about the vast majority of pain and hatred in my life, it's my dad that comes to mind. When I traced back the majority of the difficulties I have faced, and the stupid decisions I have made, it's my dad that comes to mind. Ouch. All of this internal pain made life unbearable, and I often thought that suicide would fix my problems. Thank God, I only ever thought about it, instead of attempting it. Looking back, the pain that I experienced was not going to last forever. Suicide, however, is a permanent solution to a temporary problem.

Death is forever. That is why I believe suicide is not the answer. There is a much better way to get rid of the hurt and pain.

But is love *truly* greater than hate? You can't answer that until you have faced the pain that people have caused you and the anger that you feel towards them. But let me tell you, love is greater than hate, and when you get a hold of that, it reverses the cycle of hate, breaks the back of bullying, and launches us into a new cycle where three radical changes become a new way of life. I've seen it, I have felt it, and I've experienced it myself.

2.3 THREE STEPS TO MEGA CHANGE

Choosing to live in love rather than hate, begins a cycle of change that moves from Thought —> Action—> Feeling.

STEP 1: CHANGE YOUR THOUGHTS

The beginning of change starts when you change your thinking about someone. Thoughts are very powerful. Your whole life is basically shaped by your thoughts. Someone once said, "You are not what you think you are, **but what you think, you are.**" That is, if you are going to change your life, you have to change your thought patterns in several different ways.

THOUGHTS ABOUT "SELF"

I remember on several occasions throughout my childhood looking in the mirror at my skinny white-boy body with chicken legs and analyzing my broken-out face, mouth, and tongue. (Did I mention that I was allergic to just about everything?) I would then say to my reflection, "I hate you." I wanted so badly to be someone else. I wanted to be strong, handsome, and popular. I wanted to make other people believe that I was better, cooler, and more talented than I really was. But I had no power to become so, and instead, I began to exaggerate my accomplishments and downright lie about who I was and what I had done. In fact, I became *addicted* to lying to try to get people to love me, but the bullies just wouldn't let up. What could I do?

It has been said that the TRUTH will set you free. I know this to be absolutely true in my own life. When you live in truth, you simply evaluate exactly what the bully said or did and expose the lies. If the bully said that you were worthless, Truth tells you that this is a lie. You have immeasurable value. If the bully said that you were fat, and that hurt you because you felt that they spoke truth... it was a lie. You may be overweight, but FAT is not who you are. You are not your body. You are not your fat. You are not any disability that your body possesses. Speak that truth to yourself. Write out the lies. If you were physically, verbally, or sexually abused by someone you trust, expose those lies on paper as well. Take all the lies then speak out against them by saying something like this to yourself:

> *"It was wrong to hurt me in that way. I didn't deserve what you did. You should have never treated me the way you did. You should have protected me rather than hurt me. You should have respected me as a human being, and not taken advantage of me. You were in the wrong, and I will never allow myself to be hurt in the way that you hurt me."*

THOUGHTS ABOUT THE ONES WHO HURT YOU

Change always begins with new thinking, and if you want to be free from your anger, and to start to love someone—especially someone who has hurt you—you must change the way you think about them. When we hate someone, often times we make them into an evil monster in our minds. We see them as worse than they really are. Their mistakes are magnified in our head and we are blind to any good that they might try to do. This is the danger of harboring bad thoughts towards others: *Your imagination will often turn your bad thoughts into worse more hateful thoughts.*

I really experienced this with my dad. When I started thinking about all the things that he did wrong, and when I added up in my head all of the broken promises that he made to me and my sister, I was infuriated with him. The more I dwelled on those hurtful thoughts, the more I poisoned my mind with hate. My dad eventually became an evil, monster-like figure in my head. I thought he was totally callous, didn't care or love us, and only lived for himself. But it wasn't true, even though it *felt* true. Listen, feelings don't like the truth. They feed off of sensational lies and exaggerations. Your feelings are often like talk-show hosts looking for a juicy bit of gossip to chew on. It brings satisfaction of some sort.

I have found the quickest way to curb my manipulative emotions is to ground my feelings in truth. I get a grip on my thinking, and speak the truth to myself. "This is exactly what is going on. I will not be overly dramatic, and I refuse to hang onto negative thoughts towards those who hurt me."

STOP THINKING OF BULLIES AS "BAD GUYS"

Do you want to stop being a victim? Then starting right now, get rid of the idea that bullies are "the bad guys" and their victims are "the good guys." Of course, that's not easy to do. Your teachers and parents tell you bullies are bad. But as long as you think bullies are bad, you are going to hate them and treat them like enemies. So they will continue to *be* your enemies—and continue to win.

It may seem obvious that bullies are bad and you are good. But do you think your bullies see it that way? I bet they think they're the good guys and you're the bad one. Who is to say you are right and they are wrong?

Whenever you are angry, you feel like a *victim*. But those you are angry at feel you are a *bully* because your anger is the desire to scare them off or beat them up. So if you go around being angry at your bullies, you probably look like a bad guy.

In fact, many victims are actually accused of being the real bullies. Has this ever happened to you? If so, it probably made you furious because you felt it was unfair. (And your fury makes you look even more like the *real* bad guy). Since you don't like it when others think of you as a bad guy, you have to stop thinking of others as bad guys.

There's an easy way to determine if people who bother you feel they're your bully or your victim. Ask yourself: *Are they angry with me?* If they are, you can be sure they don't like how you are treating them—they feel you are bullying them. This is actually what goes on in most conflicts. Both sides are angry, and each one thinks it's the innocent victim and the other is the guilty bully. *True* bullies—those who don't see themselves as victims—are not angry. They are cool and confident while their victims walk around feeling angry.

There are kids who are mean to others and have no friends at all. They may look like bullies, but they are not. They feel like colossal victims. They are so mad at everybody for not liking them; all they want to do is get even. If you know people like that, they need help. (Make sure they read this book!)

It's easy to think of bullies as abnormal, evil creatures designed to hurt us and ruin our lives. The truth is they really are not that different from the rest of us. They want exactly what we want: to be winners in life. We all want power. We all want respect. And we all want to be popular. The difference between bullies and their victims is that the bullies are better at getting what they want. Thinking of people as good guys and bad guys may help us feel better, but it is much more helpful to think of people as winners and losers.

Just about everyone we call bullies are buddies to their friends. Bullies protect their buddies and enjoy being tough enough to stand up against others. If they thought of you as a friend, they would fight for you, too!

We may not want to admit it, but bullies tend to have a trait we admire: courage. What they do may not be smart, but they have the guts to challenge other people. Of course, it doesn't take much courage to pick on smaller and weaker kids, but many bullies stand up to bigger and stronger kids, too. They are even willing to risk punishment from adults who take the side of the victims.

START THINKING OF BULLIES AS "GOOD GUYS"

To turn your bullies into buddies, you have to start thinking of them as "good guys." Strange as it may sound, I want you to tell yourself they are doing you a favor when they bully you.

You may be thinking, *"Are you nuts? They're doing me a favor when they bully me? They're destroying my life!"*

I know it sounds crazy. But think for a minute about professional boxers. Boxers want to become great fighters and develop the skills to win. Do you think they will ever succeed without someone to spar against? Of course not. They need sparring partners who are willing to go into the ring and slug it out with them.

Do boxers *hate* their sparring partners? Do you think they are mad at them for hitting back and trying to knock them out? Do they wish a truck would run them over so they'll never be able to hurt them again? No. They need sparring partners. Without this kind of practice, they will never become successful boxers.

The same thing is true with your bullies. Think of them as your sparring partners in the game of life, and they will help you train to be a winner. Remember, people are going to try to bully you throughout your life. The sooner you learn how to deal with them, the sooner your life as a winner will begin.

Therefore, I want you to see your bullies as your sparring partners. Be grateful to them for giving you the chance to practice your skills. If it weren't for them, you would not be reading this book and learning how to become a winner with people for the rest of your life.

Taking on bullies may not always go smoothly. You're likely to make mistakes in the beginning, but that's how life is. The professional boxer doesn't win every time. If you lose, don't get mad at the bullies. Just do your best to win the next time.

There's another reason to think of bullies as good guys. Until now they have been mean to you, so you think of them as bad. Would you feel the same way if instead of hurting you they protected you? Of course not. Your goal is to turn your bullies into buddies. When you succeed, they will indeed be good in your eyes. To start that process, all you have to do is begin thinking of them as good. The sooner you do, the quicker you'll start to win.

EXPECT THE BEST

The last step in changing your thinking is, in my opinion, the most difficult: *expecting the best in those you don't like.* If you love someone, you will always believe in him, always expect the best of him. Love expects the best. Have you noticed that we tend to live up to what people expect of us? The father who always says to his son, "You will never amount to anything; you're a loser," is setting the boy up for failure. When we expect the best, we bring out the best.

You say, "But I don't think there is anything good in my enemy." That is not true. There is good in all of us. We all have the capacity to be kind—it just needs to be drawn out of us. Your enemy needs your love. This may force you to love by faith; then so be it. You will have to believe in something that you do not see. In my opinion, *loving by faith is the greatest force in the world.* Your enemy will experience this undeserved love and be floored by it. You see, love is contagious, and it changes people. It can transform a personality!

I used to say things like: "My dad is the most selfish person I have ever met. He is cold-hearted and I hate him." That was how I felt, but it simply wasn't true. My dad did love me. He did try his best to fight his alcohol addiction, but continually failed. His broken promises were hurtful, yes, but they didn't represent his true character. He struggled to know how to be a good father because no one taught him what a good father figure looked like. He really wanted to be a good dad, but he had no idea how to raise us properly. He was simply ill-prepared and immature. That's the truth, and when I started to change my thinking based on this truth, I saw him differently.

Changing your thinking about yourself, about others, and then truly looking for the best in people is the first step of the love strategy that radically transforms your life. But that's not all there is to it! We've got two more steps to go...

STEP 2: CHANGE YOUR ACTIONS

Love isn't just changing your thinking, love also requires changing your actions. But what kind of actions? I want you to do nice things for your enemy. Consider doing things that will blow both their minds and yours. Wash their car, offer to buy them lunch, offer to help them with a project. You can turn your enemy into a friend by showing yourself to be friendly.

When someone is nice to us, we feel like being nice back. When someone is mean to us, we feel like being mean back. Nobody taught this to us; it's the way we are designed. Mother Nature programmed us to treat other people the way they treat us. That's because thousands of years ago in the caveman days, we had plenty of real enemies that wanted to hurt or kill us. If others were nice to us, it was smart to be their friends in return. It made both of us stronger, especially when there were enemies around that wanted to demolish us. But those who were mean to us were probably looking to hurt or kill us, so it made sense to be even meaner to them than they were to us.

A long time ago, someone had a brilliant idea. If it's our nature to treat others the way they treat us, it must also be *their* nature to treat us the way we treat them. Who needs enemies? Enemies hurt us and make us miserable. So why not force everyone to become our friends? All we have to do is treat others nicely even when they are being mean to us. Before long, they will start treating us back nicely because they are programmed to treat us the way we treat them!

This concept has become known as The Golden Rule: "Treat others as you would like to be treated." This rule is so wonderful that every religion has adopted it in some form, such as, "Love your neighbor as yourself," and "Whatever is hateful to you, do not to others." The Golden Rule is the ultimate rule for having success in civilization. Since civilization provides enough food for everyone, we don't have to be enemies at all. By using The Golden Rule, everyone becomes friends and we all become stronger and happier.

Throughout your life, if you are ever unsure about how to handle a problem with another person, ask yourself if you are using The Golden Rule: *"Am I treating this person the way I would like to be treated?"* or *"Would I like it if they were doing to me what I am doing to them?"* If the answer is "Yes," you will probably solve the problem. If the answer is "No," you will probably get bad results and should change your strategy.

Here is another tip that just might convert your enemy into a friend (or at least into a non-enemy). It doesn't always work, but I have seen it in action and it just might work for you. If the person bullying you just won't stop and you are daily feeling the need to avoid them, do this: Write a hand written note of apology to them. Seriously, hear me out. This is brilliant and it almost always works.

Write something like this:

"Hey (insert their name), I just wanted to write a quick note of apology. I have been really angry with you lately. I have felt that you are mistreating me. To be honest, my anger has really gotten out of control. I don't like the fact that I have such bad feelings towards you. Before my feelings get out of hand, I need to sincerely apologize. I am sorry for my anger. You don't deserve to be hated or mistreated by me. I will commit to trying to treat you with respect. I would appreciate it if you would also make an effort to show me the same kindness.

In my heart of hearts, I know that you are a good person. I promise to control my thoughts and not allow anger to come between us again. Thanks for reading, (your name).

Remember that bullies are hurting people who hurt people in order to defend and feel better about themselves. Their issue may not even be with you. It may be deep-seated anger that they have towards someone *else*. So lead by example. Show them how you deal with your anger through apology and kindness. They will observe your maturity and be humbled by your response. If for some reason, they still won't stop their mean behavior; try not to take things too personal. They have deep anger issues that need special attention from an expert. If the bully consistently targets you, seek out a trusted adult to resolve the conflict. You have done everything you can do, and now you need a grown-up to intervene. That's what adults are there for, to protect and take care of you. (They probably pay your car insurance too, but that's beside the point.)

Don't let the bully mess with your head and torment you. They have a problem bigger than you.

CHANGE WHAT YOU SAY

Some people claim that they have a right to say anything they want. They hide behind their first amendment right to "Free Speech."

Please don't get me wrong, I am a massive supporter for people speaking their mind. However "free speech" crosses over the line into "hate speech" when people or people groups are personally threatened. This is what bullying is all about: physical or verbal bashing. It is so easy to cross that line.

You have to really think before you speak. Before you say something that might be hateful, ask yourself these questions:

Is it true?

Is it necessary?

Is it kind?

Put your words through this filter process. If it can't get past *true, necessary, or kind*—DON'T SAY IT! There is a respectable way to debate ideas or share disagreements. You don't call names; you don't exaggerate or manipulate facts to present an untrue picture of the targeted person. When you disagree with someone, you honor them as if they are still in the room with you.

When I am hurt by someone, it is wrong to complain to others about my pain to get sympathy. Worse yet, sometimes I might use words to encourage others to hate my enemy. *"Did you hear what Biff the school bully told me today? Can you believe how mean and insensitive he is? The dude doesn't have a caring bone in his body. I can't stand the guy..."* Be careful not to cross the line of gossip and slander when speaking to others about your enemy. You'll need to bite your tongue in order to stop talking about how wrong they are and how evil they are. By changing what you say, you are not living in the past anymore—you are changing your thoughts about them and choosing to leave the drama behind. That's living above the line. I know, I know: that's not what everybody else does... but that's the point. Just because the mainstream culture seems to be dishing out angry words doesn't make it right for you to do it to someone else.

My hope is that you would start showing the world around you that hateful speech is wrong, and refuse to disrespect people with your words or actions. When you do this, you show incredible maturity, and you give us all hope for a brighter future.

CHANGE WHAT You Do

Okay, just in case you don't think I'm totally insane yet, let me share with you what I think is a vital change that must be made if we are to win the war against bullying. Ready for this one? *Return Love for Hate.* That's right. Break the hatred cycle with a hammer of love.

Love is a verb. It is supposed to have an element of action. When you love someone, you show them your love by doing things that bring them happiness. You say, "Brooks, are you telling me that I have to do nice things to the person I don't even like, even to bullies?" Yes. Yes this is what I am asking, and this is exactly what you will be doing, because I know that you want to move past your anger and hate and climb to a higher level of living.

So, how do we show love towards our enemies?

- We must overlook their faults.

- We can look for things to give to them.

- We discover their needs and respond to them.

- We help them in practical ways.

- We can do them a favor.

- When they curse us, we bless them.

- When they knock us down, we lift them up.

- When they discourage us, we encourage them.

And, if you are a person of faith, you can pray for them. I personally believe that prayer is an incredible tool. Ask God to change your relationship with your enemy. You can pray for good things to happen to those who hurt you. Perhaps so many good things will happen to your enemy that they will desire to stop hurting others. But even if they don't change right away, praying for them will change your attitude toward them. Praying for people not only changes them, but it changes us too. This is love in action, plain and simple.

Returning love for hate is one of the greatest secrets I know. Treat the person that has hurt you the way you want him or her to become. That is how you change another person. Do you want your enemy to be kind? Treat them as if they are. Do you want them to stop talking bad about you? Treat them with respect. Speak well to them and of them, and they could very well do the same to you. This is not to be done in a manipulative way, but in a genuine way that strives to see the best in them. Love expects the best.

Hey, I know that every molecule in your body is screaming "But I don't *feel* like it! It will be *more* painful to do something nice to them!

I would rather just live with the pain, than to show loving actions towards them!" So, let's take a minute and figure out what to do with those feelings.

Step 3: Change Your Feelings

Listen, I never said living above the line is easy. It's really, really hard to show kindness to someone who has hurt you. It doesn't seem fair. You will at first feel like a fake... and my encouragement to you is to simply "fake it 'til you feel it." Usually, we only want to love those people that we feel love towards. *But I believe that you can't wait for the feelings of love before you show love.* You simply have to start thinking loving thoughts, showing loving actions, and then loving feelings will follow.

So if you want to change your feelings, you have to first change your thinking. You can't just decide, hey, *I am going to change my feelings today.* It is *not* possible to just change your feelings in a snap. Anger, worry, resentment, etc... these are all negative emotions/feelings that are just reacting to negative thoughts. If you wait until you feel like loving before you act in love, it's never going to happen. That's backwards. Get this: *It is easier to act my way into a feeling than to feel my way into an action.* If I act as if I'm enthusiastic, I will soon begin to feel enthusiastic. If I act as if I'm happy, before you know it I will feel happy. Try right now putting the biggest smile on your face that you can muster up; then make yourself laugh—really laugh inside. At first it will seem forced, but dig deep and create the body movement of laughter. You *will* begin to feel happier. (You're smiling right now, aren't you! I can tell.) If we begin to act lovingly, we will soon feel loving. *Feelings follow action.*

When I was taking pilot lessons, my instructor taught me how to put the plane in automatic pilot mode. I set the plane to head east all by itself, and it was incredible to see this big plane go in whatever direction I programmed it to go. When my instructor then told me to make a 180-degree turn in the opposite direction, the natural thing to do was grab the steering wheel and turn the plane by sheer force.

But the whole time I was fighting the auto pilot. Even if I successfully changed course, the moment I let go of the wheel, the plane would automatically return to its original programmed direction.

This is exactly how our feelings work. Trying to change our feelings by sheer will-power will leave us exhausted and defeated. You can't just psych your feelings into loving someone you hate. Feelings don't work like that. They are automatically responding to the brains computer which is programmed to tell it where to go.

The best way to change the direction of the plane was to simply re-program the automatic pilot. That is exactly what I did. No sense fighting the plane's powerful computer—and there is no sense fighting your own brain either. The "Automatic Pilot" in your life is your thoughts. **Where your thoughts go, your feelings follow.** So if you want to change your feelings, reprogram your thoughts. I can't tell you how powerful this principle is. Stop thinking the thoughts that are getting you into trouble and start thinking thoughts that will get you where you want to go.

Remember, you can't change your feelings directly. You have to first change your thoughts, *then* your actions, and *then* your feelings will change!

If you do what I am suggesting here, I guarantee that you will change your feelings toward those who hurt you. You will feel sorry for their pain. You will start to understand why they are the way they are. You will pity their struggle. Love will open your eyes. You will gain the ability to see past their masks of hate and see a heart full of hurt. The more you think and act in love, the more your feelings will erupt in genuine care for that person. In fact, you will blow yourself away when you realize how much you wish your enemy well. This is the final sign of healing, and it snaps the cycle of hatred.

2.4 THE POWER OF FORGIVENESS

If you *really* want to change your painful thoughts of hate, then you need to take one last step: you must forgive those who have hurt you.

I can't tell you how important this is, but after you've experienced it, you'll understand. "Forgiveness" is another word that is commonly misunderstood. When I talk to teens about forgiveness, they often get squeamish and shy. It sounds too deep, psychological, or religious to them.

It's not that complicated. Forgiveness simply put is: **releasing the person that did you wrong from the responsibility of fixing it.** When you forgive, you are basically saying in your heart and mind:

"Bully, what you did was wrong. It hurt me and has negatively affected my life. But what's done is done. You can't take it back or change the past. I must move on with my life, so I release you from the responsibility to fix my life. Because you can't. I forgive you for hurting me. I free you from my anger. I no longer resent you. I will learn from the pain, and become a better person because of it."

Some young people actually enjoy their anger. They feel that the anger is like a prison in their mind that locks up people they don't like. They are afraid that if they forgive someone completely, it will let that person out of the prison and off the hook. They don't want to see that bully go free. One way or another, bullies will pay the price for their actions. The problem is that unforgiveness locks us up in our own prison of anger and hate, and we become chained to our pain. The cool thing is that getting free is totally within our control.

Forgiveness is a choice. It is in your power right now to forgive your enemy. You shouldn't wait for the person to apologize or change their behavior—you must forgive them in your heart and mind as soon as possible. I believe that when you allow the bully to stay in your mind through angry thoughts and feelings, the bully is winning and you are losing. It is as if the bully is controlling you from the inside of the cell of your mind, keeping you from happiness and stealing your personality. When you forgive, however, all of that is released. The chains of the past fall away and you have the freedom to live and love like never before.

In order to get there, however, you might have to overcome some common misunderstandings about forgiveness:

- Many people feel that if they forgive, they have to forget. They think that if they forgive they are denying that the painful event ever happened. Not so. You were hurt by someone and I would never expect you to deny that fact.

- Many people feel that if they forgive, they might also forget and be put in the same situation again. Not so. I am not asking you to forgive and forget. I am just asking you to forgive. Remember, we need to live in truth. Truth doesn't let us just forget what happened, because we should not forget. Living in truth demands that we remember exactly what happened. Truth has a way of making us "street-smart" and keeps us from being hurt the same way twice. When you combine truth with forgiveness, you have an awesome combination. You are able to remember the hurtful event, remember how much it effected you, but then move forward without lingering hatred or anger towards that person. You have forgiven them and are moving on! Living in forgiveness will set you free, living in truth will keep you smart.

- Some people are afraid that if they choose forgiveness, they are basically saying that it was okay that the bully hurt them. This is also wrong. It was not okay, and is never okay for someone to hurt you. It is wrong. Forgiveness doesn't mean that you have to approve of the wrongdoing.

- Some people want the bully to come crawling to them asking for forgiveness before they are willing to grant it. Listen to me very carefully, you can't wait for the person that hurt you to apologize or change their ways. If you wait for them, you will continue to hurt forever and the hurt will grow into hate and eventually hijack your happiness forever. Trust me.

- Some people think that they have to confront their bully face to face. The thought of speaking to them turns their stomach. The good news is that you don't have to confront them. Forgiveness is something that you do internally, in your heart and mind. Sometimes it helps to forgive the person face to face, but it isn't necessary. Get this, **forgiveness is not for them anyways. It is for you!** It frees you from the conflict and empowers you to move on.

Finally, many of us wrestle with this thought: "But they don't deserve forgiveness! They hurt me too bad." Believe me, I understand pain. It hurts. People can do and say the most hurtful things. But let me remind you that you are not exactly an angel. Remember what I told you earlier, you are a bully too. There have been people you have hurt. You have said things to others that have devastated them. You may not be as bad of a bully as the bullies who have hurt you, but friend, you have still done bad things. So please, don't buy into the lie that someone is too bad or too hurtful to deserve forgiveness. Because I imagine someone could say the same about you. The people you have hurt could continue to harbor resentment towards you. That wouldn't be cool would it? Wouldn't you love to be released from the responsibility to fix what you have done? That is what forgiveness is all about. It is undeserved grace. It is a "get out of jail" card for the one who deserves to be locked up. It is kindness extended to the bully who doesn't deserve it.

Forgiveness is totally illogical to the human mind, but something in your soul knows that it is the right thing to do, doesn't it. It is going to take incredible courage to lay down your anger once and for all, and choose to forgive. It may be one of the hardest experiences of your life. But let me tell you from my own experience, it will give you your life back. Forgiveness really is a choice. It is not something that happens over time, gradually. Forgiveness only happens by choice at a moment in time. A moment just like NOW. Today. My friend, you are about to have a breakthrough. I can feel it, even as I write this.

Would you be willing to take a leap of faith with me right now? Grab some paper and something to write with, and then write three things:

1. **The Offense.** I want to challenge you right now to write about the pain that has been inflicted on you. Go into as much detail as you need. Let the tears flow if they want to.

2. **The Truth.** Write down why this was wrong, and what should have been the right thing for them to do or say.

3. **The Forgiveness.** Then write a short statement of forgiveness to the people who caused it. Say their names out loud to yourself and tell them that you release them from the responsibility to fix what they did. Tell them what they said was not all true. They were wrong to say what they said and do what they did. Then commit to them that you will no longer harbor angry thoughts about them.

This is how it looked when I did this about my dad:

The Offense:

Dad, you left me when I was young. You caused me so much pain with your alcohol addiction and your inability to be there for me when I needed you.

The Truth:

I deserved a father figure who would never leave me or forsake me. You should have been a better example to me. I have learned, from your mistakes, on how not to live my life.

The Forgiveness:

Dad, I forgive you for hurting me so deeply. There is nothing you can do to fix what you have done, so I release you from my anger. I no longer look to you with hatred. I am in charge of my own life now, and I am moving on. I hope we can have a better relationship now that I am slowly being healed, one day at a time.

So you write the stuff down, and then, let it go. You might want to tear up what you have written as a symbol that you are moving on, or you might want to keep it as a reminder to your feelings that you are choosing to forgive even when it doesn't feel right. Either way, never bring it up in your relationship with them or allow your mind to dwell on that pain again. You are uprooting the pain from the deepest part of your heart and casting it away. You might need to talk with a counselor or pastor or maybe even the police about what happened, but you are breaking the anger/hatred cycle and setting your heart free with love.

I am living proof that this stuff works. If you are able to uproot the hatred that you feel towards others, and really deal with the hurt that is deep within, then you can experience freedom from the bondage of hate. I personally have experienced massive healing from my hurtful past.

I no longer feel any anger towards my dad. I have the most intense love for him, and our relationship now is vibrant. I have totally forgiven the people who have spent years harassing me in school. I don't hold any grudges or have any hard feelings towards anyone. That is the truth about me. And guess what? You can experience the same thing! You don't need to hold on to any pain or sadness from your past. You can totally rise above the hurt, lay down the hatred, and become the loving person that you have dreamed about being. When you do this, you are uprooting the pain from the deepest part of your heart and casting it away.

What a powerful opportunity you have right now to change your life through the power of love, forgiveness and truth.

Do it. Now.

WORK IT OUT

THE OFFENSE:
How were you hurt?

THE TRUTH:
Why was this wrong?

THE FORGIVENESS:
Release them from your anger and their responsibility to fix it.

WORK IT OUT

THE OFFENSE:
How were you hurt?

THE TRUTH:
Why was this wrong?

THE FORGIVENESS:
Release them from your anger and their responsibility to fix it.

WORK IT OUT

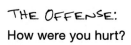

THE OFFENSE:
How were you hurt?

THE TRUTH:
Why was this wrong?

THE FORGIVENESS:
Release them from your anger and their responsibility to fix it.

Once you have taken this courageous step, you're ready to jump into the next chapter and be a powerful force of change on your campus.

THE CHALLENGE:
RESPONDING TO BULLIES

Now that you have gone through the incredible process of learning to love and forgive the bully in your life, you may face the challenge of treating them with respect day in and day out. This can be really hard if they haven't changed the way they treat you. I don't want you to resort back to hate once you have practiced loving them. You must learn how to love them even when they continually try and hurt your feelings. This may sound difficult, but don't worry! You are about to discover a strategy that will help you interact with an enemy who is a constant challenge to love.

I have a good friend and mentor named Izzy Kalman. As a school psychologist, he has been helping students become bully-proof for years. He has graciously allowed me to share with you his secret rules that have the power to turn your "bullies into buddies."

TURNING BULLIES INTO BUDDIES: THE SECRET

This is how you will:

1. Prevent yourself from having enemies

2. Stop people from fighting with you

3. Turn yourself into a winner

4. Get more respect

These rules will work with anyone. They work with other kids. They'll work with brothers and sisters. You can even use them on your parents. Each rule will be explained in a section of its own.

Rule 1: Refuse to get mad.

Rule 2: Treat everything as the words of your best friend.

Rule 3: Don't be afraid of bullies.

Rule 4: Don't attack bullies.

Rule 5: Don't defend yourself.

Rule 6: Don't tell on bullies.

Rule 7: Show you are hurt, not angry.

3.1 REFUSE TO GET MAD

Question: Is anger a feeling we have toward friends or enemies?

Answer: Anger is not a nice, pleasant, friendly feeling. It is what we feel toward an enemy. We feel we are being attacked and we want to scare or hurt our opponent. Even when we're mad at good friends, at that moment we feel they are acting like our enemies. This makes them mad right back at us, so they treat us like an enemy, too.

Question: When someone bothers us and we get mad, who is the loser?

Answer: We are. To defeat us, people don't have to break our bones or make us bleed. All they have to do is make us mad. When we are mad, we feel miserable and they feel good. Since everyone wants to win, they will keep on doing exactly what gets us mad.

Because we don't want to turn people into enemies, and we don't want to be losers, we have to refuse to give them the power to make us angry.

You may be thinking, *"But how can I just decide to stop being mad and upset when people are mean to me?"*

When people treat us badly, we get angry. This is an automatic response programmed into our brains. It feels like our bullies have a remote control to our brain and they're pressing the "anger button" to make us mad.

But bullies do not really push buttons to control our brains. It just feels like that because of the way Mother Nature programmed us. She gave us the automatic response of getting angry to help us against enemies when we were living in the dangerous world of nature. When you get mad, do you *decide* to get mad? Do you tell yourself, *"I think getting angry is the smart thing to do in this situation because it will help me win"?* No, of course not. Since you get angry without thinking about it, it feels like others make you angry.

Today we live in civilization, where life is much safer. We don't have to hunt or fight to survive. In fact, there are very strict laws against fighting, so there is a good chance that fighting will get us in deep trouble.

You may *want* to punch your bullies in the nose, but you are not allowed to. Your opponents can do all kinds of things to get you mad without being afraid that you will hurt them. They can laugh while you get angrier and angrier. The angrier you get, the more you become the loser.

So tell yourself the only way to win is by *not* getting mad! Disable the "anger button" in your brain. Show your bullies they can try all they want, but they can't get you mad! This is really not so hard to do once you realize it. There are many things our bodies do without our awareness but we can still control them if we wish. When you see something funny, your automatic response is to laugh, but you can easily stop yourself from laughing. If a doctor tests your reflexes by tapping below your knee with a hammer, your leg will automatically respond by kicking, but you can decide not to let your leg kick. When people are mean to you, the natural response is to get angry, but you can decide not to.

It will be easier to control your anger if you get rid of the idea that bullies "have no right" to be mean to you. Of course, they don't have the right to commit *crimes* against you, like injuring you or stealing from you, but there is no law forcing them to be *nice*. If you believe that people have no right to be mean to you, you will become angry whenever they aren't nice. But if you realize people *do* have a right to be mean, you won't automatically get mad when they are nasty.

When you refuse to get mad, your bullies will discover they can no longer defeat you. They will feel like fools and losers every time they pick on you. Before long, they won't even *try* to get you upset because they don't want to lose. You will become the winner without doing anything against them. And you will get respect, because you are the winner, not the loser.

Another strange thing will happen. The bullies will start liking you better when they see they can't defeat you. Why? For three basic reasons:

1. *You are no longer mad at them.* People don't like you when you are mad at them. When you stop being angry, they won't have a reason to be angry either.

2. *They can respect you now.* You want friends you can respect. Your bullies are no different. If you get mad, they can't respect you because you are the loser. When they can no longer defeat you, they will respect you more. Then it will be much easier for them to become your friends.

3. *You are showing them respect.* Your bullies enjoy respect just as much as you do. When you no longer get angry, you are treating the bullies with more respect. And they will like you better for it!

3.2 TREAT EVERYTHING AS THE WORDS OF YOUR BEST FRIEND

This is an absolutely wonderful and powerful rule for having good relationships. It sounds kind of crazy, but it works beautifully and you should use it with everyone in your life. Tell yourself that everything people tell you, no matter how nasty or angry they sound, is the words of your best friend. Tell yourself that the only reason they are talking to you like this is because they love you, care about you, and want to help you.

This doesn't mean you have to treat them as if they are right, or that you have to do whatever they tell you. All it means is that you consider them to have nothing but good intentions. Be grateful for everything they have to say to you.

If someone calls you stupid, tell yourself they are saying it not because they want to hurt your feelings but because they want to help you be smarter. So how could you be mad at them? Or if they call you a fatso, it is because they are trying to encourage you to go on a diet. So be appreciative.

If your parents call you a spoiled brat, don't get mad at them. Realize they are trying to get you to act more maturely, and then it will be easier for them to give you more of what you want.

On the other hand, if people urge you to shoplift, don't do it just because you're considering them to be your best friends. Tell yourself they are trying to help you have things you can't afford, but you can't do it because it is illegal and against your beliefs.

Or if someone tells you to jump off a tall building, you shouldn't do it just because you are considering them friends who love you. But you should tell yourself they must have a very good reason for saying it. Maybe it's their way of hinting that you are acting like a jerk and would do everyone a favor by stopping.

Don't forget that your goal is to be a winner by having as many friends and as few enemies as possible. And if you *think* of people as your friends, they are more likely to *be* your friends.

3.3 Don't Be Afraid of Bullies

"What do you mean, don't be afraid of bullies? The bullies are scary! They ridicule me in front of everyone! They hurt my feelings. They threaten me and hit me!"

Question: Are we afraid of friends, or are we afraid of enemies?

Answer: Fear, of course, is something we feel toward enemies. Friends don't want to hurt us, so there's no need to fear them. Therefore, by being afraid of bullies, we are treating them like enemies. So they'll treat us like enemies. Our bullies will never stop bullying us as long as we continue to be afraid of them.

Question: If we are afraid of someone, who is in the stronger position?

Answer: The other person is. By being afraid of someone, we put ourselves in the weaker position. We automatically lose and don't get respect. Since everyone wants to be a winner, our bullies will continue doing whatever makes us afraid.

"But how can I just stop being afraid? The bullies are dangerous and can hurt me."

If we were still living in caveman days, then you would be smart to be afraid of bullies. There was real, serious fighting going on then, and no one went to jail for beating someone up.

But now we live in civilization. We have tons of rules against hurting people, and there are policemen and courts and prisons to make sure the rules are followed. When we are in school, the school staff does a pretty good job of enforcing the same rules. (Chances are you do a lot less fighting in school than you do at home with your brothers and sisters!) The law is like an invisible shield to protect us. If bullies injure us, it is easy to get them in serious trouble and they lose big time.

Don't assume that bullies are stupid. They don't want to get in trouble. But fortunately for them, there is an easy way for them to defeat you without physically hurting you. They play a game with you called "Let's Scare People." If you get scared, you lose.

It's easy for them to scare us by taking advantage of the fact that our brains still work like cavemen brains. We are programmed to respond to their threats as though they really *are* going to hurt us. In caveman times, being afraid was important for survival. Our fear kept us out of fights with people who could hurt us. While we're no longer in real danger from bullies, our brains still respond as though we are. So bullies keep on scaring us, even though they probably don't intend to injure us, and they win.

But you want to be a winner, so you must decide to stop being afraid of bullies. Even if they are bigger and stronger than you, don't worry. You aren't in real danger. Most of them are not the evil villains you have been imagining them to be. They are just playing around with you. When you stop being afraid of them, they feel foolish trying to scare you and soon stop. Then they cease being your enemies and are free to be your friends.

So when you find your body telling you, *"Oh, no, the bullies are so big and strong! I'm afraid they are going to hurt me,"* catch yourself and realize that this fear makes you automatically lose. Instead, tell yourself something like this:

"They are bigger and stronger than I am, but they can't hurt me. I'm not strong enough to beat them up by myself, but that's okay because I don't have to. There is an invisible shield protecting me, and if they go through this shield, the law is going to punish them and I am going to win. So they can act as scary as they want, and it doesn't bother me in the least!"

It's not enough just to stop being scared of people who threaten you. It is also essential not to get mad at them, either, or you'll end up enemies. So be perfectly calm. Don't give them any dirty looks. Smile instead. Tell yourself that people have every right in the world to try to scare you, and you are not going to take this right away from them.

Since they're not doing anything wrong, you have no reason to be mad at them. With this attitude, you will discover that people like you and respect you, and that you have no enemies, no matter how small or weak you may be. In fact, if you have no fear and anger, they may even admire you and want to act as your protectors, *especially* if you are small and weak! So stop being afraid of them, and you just might get yourself some free bodyguards!

Warning: *There is, of course, a chance that someone is so angry with you that he will actually try to harm you physically. How can you judge if you are in real danger or not? Very simply: by asking yourself if the person threatening you has ever injured you or anyone else before. Someone who has injured people in the past may do so again. People who go around injuring others and aren't afraid of getting in trouble are dangerous. They are more than bullies. They are criminals. With such people, your natural fear is healthy. Be afraid of them, and stay far away from them. If you must be near them, make sure you have people around who can protect you. However, if the person you are afraid of has never hurt anyone (to the best of your knowledge), then you probably don't have to worry that he will hurt you, so don't be scared.*

Making us afraid that they will hurt our bodies is not the only way people can have power over us. Another simple way is by getting us to fear what they *think* of us. We are terrified that we will look bad in the eyes of others. We want their approval, and we don't feel happy until we get it. The origin of this fear is also in nature. When we were living in tribes in the jungle, there was no Welfare Department and no homeless shelters. We all had to cooperate to survive. What the group thought of us was very important. If the tribe didn't approve of us, they would ridicule us, beat us up or abandon us, and we wouldn't survive for long.

However, in civilization there is no such danger. No matter what our friends think of us, we are going to have food to eat, a bed to sleep in, schools to learn in, and hospitals to take care of us when we are sick. Therefore our basic survival doesn't depend on what others think of us. Our bodies, though, don't know this and react as though we're still in the lawless jungle. In civilization, when we care what others think of us, we are giving them power over us for nothing. Think of it this way: If I care about what you think of *me*, but you don't care what I think of *you*, who is in a stronger position? You are, of course! I will be trying to act or dress in a way I hope you will approve of, while you are doing absolutely nothing for me. You are the one in control. It's like I'm making you my boss. I become the big loser, and losers don't get respect.

Think about the really famous, successful, or powerful people in the world. Do they care what you personally think about them? No. They live their lives the way they want. They will only do what it takes to get you to buy their products or services or, if they're politicians, to vote for them. Many celebrities will purposely behave or dress outrageously. They know we will be so impressed by their daring and originality that we will want to be like them and spend money on their performances or products.

If you want to be happy and successful, stop being concerned that others will think badly of you. All that should matter is that you are acting in a way that you think is right. To win the approval game that people play with you, tell yourself something like this:

"People can think anything they want about me, and it's perfectly OK. I don't mind if they think I'm ugly, stupid, fat, nerdy or gay. This is my life, and I'm going to live it according to my own beliefs and desires."

You will discover that the less you worry what others think of you, the happier and more powerful you become. People will actually respect you more and like you better when they can't control you, and you live by your own values rather than by theirs. As long as you are not hurting them, of course.

There's another thing you should understand about the kids who tease you.

Since they are making fun of you, it seems like they hate you for being different, and if you were just like them, they would love you.

But it only *seems* that way. The truth is they are happy you are different. Part of us wants to be the same as everyone else so that we won't stick out and be made fun of. But deep down, another part of us wants to be different from everyone so that we can feel special. If you were just like your bullies, that wouldn't please them! You would be preventing them from feeling special. And you wouldn't like it, either, because *you* wouldn't be special.

If people were all the same, life would be horribly boring. Even more importantly, the world couldn't function if everyone were the same. You need people with different abilities and characteristics to do all the different jobs that are required to keep society running. So feel different, and feel special. Love others for being different from you, and they will love you for being different from them.

By the way, did you ever hear the expression, "Opposites attract"? Well, there's a lot of truth to that. In fact, the kids who tease you may be drawn to you because they are attracted by your being so different from them. You just can't see it because they are trying to make themselves feel good by making you feel bad. So don't fall into the trap of getting upset when they make fun of your differences, and they won't continue to bother you. Maybe they'll end up being your friends because they find your differences so interesting!

3.4 Don't Attack Bullies

Question: Do we attack friends or enemies?

Answer: Attacking is something we do to enemies. If we attack bullies, even if they attacked us first, we are letting them know we consider them enemies. So we can expect them to treat us like enemies.

In nature, if an enemy attacks us and we can't escape, it becomes necessary to attack back. The alternative may be death. The instinct to attack was built into our genes from the time we were cavemen. It was necessary in order to have a chance of surviving against enemies who really wanted to harm us or kill us.

But we now live in civilization. It is against the law to hurt others. The bullies know this, and they are not trying to send us to the hospital. We don't have to counterattack in order to win because we are not in real danger from the bullies. If we attack them in return, they will want to attack back even harder. Of course, it is possible that the bullies will become scared of us and leave us alone from then on. But there is a much greater chance that the fight will just get worse, and we may get seriously hurt.

You should assume that your bullies are not stupid. They don't want to get in trouble. They want *you* to get in trouble, so they do a clever trick by using your biological instincts against you. They push you or hit you quietly when the teacher isn't looking. They hope you will instinctively get mad and attack them back so loudly that everyone notices you. You end up getting punished even though the bully started! Or they may hit you back even harder, claiming that you started. By attacking back, instead of becoming a winner, you become a king-sized loser.

Bullies feel stupid for attacking someone who isn't fighting back. It is very hard for a bully to keep on attacking you if you are doing nothing. Even though it seems like you are "letting the bullies get away with it," you are really defeating them. It also makes you look tough because you can take a push or a hit and it doesn't faze you.

There is another important principle that I want you to learn from this. Everyone thinks that in a fight, the first person to hit is the one who started the fight. The truth is that the *second* person to hit really started the fight! Does this sound nutty? But it's not. It takes two people to make a fight. When someone hits you, there is no fight yet. As you discovered in the experiment, if you do nothing back, no fight happens. It's only when you attack back that a fight erupts! So yes, even though you are the second person to hit, you actually are the one who started the fight.

Warning: *This rule does not apply if you are facing someone who is intent on injuring you no matter what you do, and you are backed in a corner with no one to rescue you. If attacking back is your only chance for preventing serious harm to yourself, of course you must do it. Please remember, though, that this is an extremely rare situation that may never happen to you. If people are truly looking to injure you, they're either criminals or you must have given them a mighty good reason for hating you—like telling on them and getting them in trouble!*

3.5 Don't Defend Yourself

Does this sound strange? It may make sense to you that attacking bullies is wrong, but why shouldn't you *defend* yourself from them? Are you to simply let them walk all over you like a doormat?

Question: Do we defend ourselves from friends or from enemies?

Answer: Obviously, we defend ourselves from enemies. We don't need to defend ourselves from friends because friends don't want to hurt us.

Therefore, if we defend ourselves from bullies, it means that we consider them enemies. So they will never be our friends.

Question: If one person is attacking and the other is defending himself, who is in the stronger position?

Answer: The attacker is in the stronger position. It is not fun to have to defend yourself. The attacker has everything to gain and the defender has everything to lose. The best the defender can hope to accomplish is to maintain his or her position. When we defend ourselves we are trying to win the conflict. However, it's impossible to win by defense. It puts the attacker on top and defender at the bottom. The harder we defend ourselves, the bigger we lose, and the bully will continue attacking to force us into the losing defensive position.

If you don't want to be the loser and you don't want to have enemies, you must decide not to defend yourself when someone attacks you. You will get more respect because you will not be the loser. The bullies will like you better because you'll be treating them like friends instead of enemies.

But won't you get hurt if you don't defend yourself?

First take into account that most of the attacks against us are verbal attacks, with words, not with sticks and stones. We certainly don't have to worry about defending ourselves from words.

When the attack is physical, of course there is a chance of getting hurt. However, you have a much greater chance of getting hurt when you defend yourself. Why? Because attacking and defending are both acts of fighting. By defending yourself, you are agreeing to participate in fighting. Defense is the weaker position. When you defend yourself, you increase the bullies' confidence. They feel they have the upper hand, so they attack you even harder. The fight escalates and you may end up hurt.

It takes two people to make a fight. When you don't defend yourself, there can't be a fight. The bullies quickly feel stupid attacking people who aren't defending themselves, and then stop trying.

Warning: *As with the previous section's rule against attacking bullies, the rule against defending yourself does not apply when the attacker is absolutely determined to harm you. In such a case, not defending yourself will make it easier for them to hurt you. So you must defend yourself to avoid being physically injured. Just remember that in almost all situations, bullies are not looking to send you to the hospital. They are trying to have power over you by making you angry, scared or miserable. Most of the things they do will not hurt you.*

3.6 Don't Tell on Bullies

Have adults been urging you to tell them when other kids tease or bully you? Have they been telling you that "Telling is not tattling"?

Please do not take such advice. Telling on bullies, except under rare circumstances, is about the worst thing you can do. The best way to make people despise you without actually committing a crime against them is by trying to get them in trouble with the authorities. This is true whether you are telling your teacher on other students, your parents on your brother or sister, your boss on a coworker, or the police on your neighbor. The harder your bullies get punished, the more intensely they are going to hate you. And they will be burning to get back at you, either by hurting you again or by getting *you* in trouble.

If it is a mistake to tell on bullies, why are the adults saying you must do it? It's because they care for kids and really want to help them. They want to be your heroes fighting off the evil bullies. They just don't realize that their efforts to help may not work. In fact, when adults try to help kids in their conflicts with each other, the fighting almost always gets worse. Since both kids want the adult on their side, they each argue even harder to convince the adult they are right and their opponent is wrong.

If you have ever told your parents or teachers on your siblings or schoolmates, you probably discovered that it doesn't help. It may feel good to have the adult on your side, but the problem continues. Maybe the bullies leave you alone for a short while after they're yelled at or punished, but before long they're picking on you again. And as long as you tell on them, they'll be telling on you.

When the adults confront your bullies, do the bullies simply say, "Oh, yes, I'm guilty. I'm sorry. I won't do it again"? Sometimes they do. But more often they start blaming you and trying to get you in trouble. If the adults are attempting to be fair, there is a good chance they will decide that you are the guilty one. And if the bullies are popular, more kids will testify for them than for you. This makes you look like the real bully. You end up in trouble and being the big loser.

Do you like it when your brother or sister tells your parents on you? Of course not! Your parents are the most important people in the world to you. You want them to love you and be on your side.

When your siblings get you in trouble with your parents, you get real mad at your siblings *and* your parents.

When you are in school, it is the same thing. The teacher is the most important person in your school day. The last thing you want is for other kids to get the teacher against you.

Well, your bullies are no different from you. When you tell on them, they'd like to see you get struck by lightning. So remember the Golden Rule. If you don't want them to tell on you, you shouldn't tell on them, either.

Do you want respect? Do you want to be a winner? Of course you do. Well, no one gets the admiration of classmates by telling the teacher on other kids. When you tell on kids who bother you, you are letting everyone know that you can't handle your bullies by yourself. You are declaring that you are weaker than they are, that they are defeating you, and that you need a grown-up's help to win. Even if you get the bullies punished, you still lose because everyone knows you can't do it by yourself. Even the teachers who help you don't truly respect you. They would admire you much more if you solved your bully problem on your own. In fact, people will respect you more if you deal with bullies by yourself and lose than if you get an adult to defeat them for you. So when you tell on bullies, you look like a loser, and losers don't get respect.

There are only two instances when you should tell on people: If they have committed a crime, or to prevent a crime. By a crime I mean something that actually causes harm to someone's body or possessions. No one has a right to make you bleed or break your bones. For this they should be punished so they won't want to do it again. They are not allowed to break or steal your possessions. If they do, and are not willing to pay you back or return the items, then you should tell the authorities. If you have good reason to believe that someone is going to harm someone else, then it may be necessary to tell the authorities so they can prevent the crime from happening.

But don't try to get kids in trouble for hurting your feelings. It is not a crime. Whether your feelings are hurt depends upon you, not the other people, so it is wrong to punish them. Don't tell on them if they call you names, spread rumors, or hit you without harming you. (In later sections you will learn how to handle these situations effectively).

But there is someone you *should* tell if a bully does something you don't like. Who? The bully himself. Think of it this way. Let's say you did something to me that hurt. When will you like me better? If I tell the authorities, or if I tell *you*? Of course you would prefer that I tell you instead of trying to get you in trouble. You will respect me more for having the guts or the decency to talk to you, and you will like me more for not trying to get you in trouble. You are much more likely to apologize and stop bothering me if I tell you than if I tell your teacher, parent, or a policeman. Well, the bullies are just like you. If you need to tell, tell the bully, not the authorities. Just be sure that when you talk to the bully, you are not angry or threatening. Talk the way you would to a good friend. I can't guarantee that your bullies will always listen to you, but I can assure you that the results will be better if you tell them than if you tell *on* them.

3.7 Show You Are Hurt, Not Angry

It happens all the time. People hurt us and we get angry. But instead of apologizing and never hurting us again, they get mad and keep hurting us. Why?

If people hurt you, how do you want them to feel about it? You want them to feel *sorry*. You want them to apologize and say they won't do it again. Then you can forgive them and go on being friends.

If you get mad at the people who hurt you, you show them *anger*. So they will probably respond with anger. Do you want people to be *angry* with you when they hurt you? No, of course not. You want them to be *sorry*. But when you get mad, instead of making them feel sorry, you make them feel like they're under attack, so they get angry right back.

Why do we make this mistake? Because it is programmed into us by Mother Nature herself. As cavemen, if you hurt me there was a very good chance you would hurt me even more. Maybe you were trying to beat me up and take over my position in the tribe. Or maybe you were a wild animal trying to make me your breakfast. I had to get angry to scare you off or to tear you to pieces before you tore me to pieces. Because it helped us survive, Mother Nature made sure that we would get angry when another creature caused us pain.

But we now live in civilization. You are not an enemy looking to eat me. The law forbids you from injuring me; and if you do injure me, it is probably an accident. Getting angry at you will not do me any good. Just the opposite: It will make you angry back and we may end up enemies.

From now on, if people hurt you, do not make the mistake of getting angry. Just let them know that you are hurt. They will probably feel bad for hurting you. Then they will apologize and avoid hurting you again, which is exactly what you want.

This rule works well with friends, relatives and people who care about you. Kids who have been angry at you for a long time may be happy to see that you are hurt and will want to hurt you again. What should you do about them?

Until now, you have been in a state of war with your bullies. If you have been mad at them, they are mad at you; and if you have been telling on them, they hate you. They may want to make you suffer *now*, but they won't feel this way forever. When you turn your bullies into buddies, they will stop taking pleasure in your pain.

To get the right effect, it has to be clear that you are in serious pain and not just feeling sorry for yourself. If you are able to talk at the time, look the bully in the eyes, imagine him or her to be your best friend, and say something like, "That really hurt." But don't sound angry or the bullies will not feel sorry for hurting you. Don't cry like a baby or sadly walk away like a puppy with its tail between its legs, either. This will make you look like a wimp and a loser, and they will not care about you.

Remember, most bullies are really not heartless. They are basically no different from you and me. They do not enjoy injuring people who aren't trying to hurt them. They simply want to have power. They don't have a remote control to your brain that forces you to feel bad. When they say things and your feelings get hurt, you are really hurting yourself. Stop doing it. It's not fair to blame them when you hurt yourself; they are right to have little sympathy for you. However, if they make you bleed or break your bones, they probably feel terrible. So let your bully know you are hurt when the pain is physical.

3.8 THREE POINTS TO REMEMBER

To succeed in turning your bullies into buddies you need to avoid falling into traps that will make the bullying continue.

1. The bullying will get worse before it gets better.

Wouldn't it be wonderful if all you had to do is read this book and then you would never be picked on again? Well, it's almost that simple, but not quite. In fact, you must be prepared for the bullying to get *worse* before it gets better...but only for a couple of days.

When you change your attitude, your tormentors will discover you aren't getting upset. They'll feel confused. They'll think something is terribly wrong with you. Maybe you went blind and don't see them. Maybe you went deaf and don't hear them. They won't like the sensation that they aren't winning. But they really *want* to upset you, so they will probably try even harder. They figure if they annoy you long enough, eventually they'll get to you.

After a while, they will become tired of feeling stupid and will stop bothering you. A little later they will try again, hoping you are back to your old self and will get upset. Again, it won't work.

So when you see the harassment intensifying, don't think, *"Oh, no, this isn't working! The bullying is only getting worse!"* It *is* working. It's just that your bullies have been upsetting you for a long time, and they don't want the fun to end. Plus, you have been letting them know all along that the bullying bothers you, and they need some time to figure out that it doesn't anymore.

2. You must follow these instructions 100% of the time.

The only way to succeed in stopping your tormentors is to follow the instructions in this book—all the time. If bullies see you get upset even only once in while, they will know bullying really does bother you; they just have to try harder and more often. So the abuse won't stop. It may even get worse. Only when bullies learn they can *never* get you upset will they stop trying to bother you altogether.

3. Bullies won't disappear.

Follow the instructions in this book and your situation will improve dramatically. But don't expect you'll never get picked on again in your life. Everyone gets picked on once in a while, and there's nothing in the world we can do to change that. The difference is that it will happen much less often than it used to, and the same individual won't bother you more than once or twice. Most importantly, it won't upset you. In fact, it may even make you laugh.

You have learned how to love and forgive your enemies. You have also learned super practical ways to treat the bully in your life as a friend. Now I want you to discover how you can be a powerful force of change on your campus!

4.0

THE CHANGE STRATEGY: SEVEN DAYS TO LIFE CHANGE

The last month of my senior year came quicker than I had expected. It seemed like yesterday that I was entering high school as a freshman with a sore shoulder. I never forgot the hate that the big football player showed me on my first day. I also knew that I would always remember the friends and companions who joined together to make our school a better place. As we headed toward graduation, I knew those four years of high school were some of the most important and powerful years of my life. One spring day, as we were winding down and starting to look toward life outside of high school, some of my friends ran up to me with a newspaper in their hands. "Brooks! Did you read the paper? You're the cover story!"

What? How did I make the school newspaper? Sure enough, as I started reading, the editor of the newspaper (a fellow senior) did a feature article on me. This was a total surprise. The article was entitled, "I Aspire to be a Flyer..." (Hey, I was just glad I wasn't in the Police Blotter!) The writer described his experience of watching me enter as a freshman and graduate as a senior. He described in great detail ways that I was a bright light of love on our campus. He told the readers that they all needed to follow my example of compassion and kindness so that the school would be a better place. One of his lines read, "Brooks isn't afraid of who he is, and he's not afraid to tell you what he stands for! He has made this school better. He has more compassion in his pinky than most of us do in our whole bodies. He has clear vision for this school, and we all are inspired by it."

Wow. It took my breath away to have such wonderful things said about me. When I was reading the article for the first time I had an unbelievable sense of satisfaction—a sense that I had been part of something bigger than myself, that I had invested those years in something that really mattered. The hard work that it took to make a positive impact on my school finally paid off... and I really believe that it will pay off for you too if you are willing to work hard towards a specific goal.

Yes, my life changed a lot in high school, but I think that article changed me for the rest of my life. I knew that what had happened in my school could happen everywhere, and I wanted to be part of making that happen.

And that's what this chapter is all about. It's a call to change your life in a way that can change your school and the world. I'm asking for seven days from you; give me a week and we can change your life forever. Not only can we help you and your friends combat the issue on your campus; but we will create a written plan of action for the rest of your life. Seriously, this might be the most important thing you do—*ever.* That's why I created something that you can work through and use immediately. I call it the "Change Strategy." This will provide a practical formula for you to bring about change in your school and your life. The strategy is made up of three distinct parts: your Big Dream, your Core Values, and your Daily Choices. Each phase in the strategy feeds off of each other. So the more you work through it, the better.

The Big Dream Phase: I will help you write an "I have a dream" speech that articulates exactly what you want to see happen on your campus. Then I will help you write a personal mission statement that will give you a personal role to play in this Big Dream. **You will be inspired to drive your life towards a clear destination.**

The Core Values Phase: I will help you choose three words that will define your personality/character. You will obsessively pursue them, and will write an affirmation statement that you will review every day. Other people will start to see you living these values out, and be inspired by you. **These core values will be the fuel that helps you arrive at your dream destination.**

The Daily Choices Phase: I will help you draw up specific and measurable goals with deadlines. This is the only way you will ever make progress towards your dreams. If you don't make daily choices that help you reach your goals, you will delay your dream ever coming to reality. I will give you great ideas on how to stay focused and make right choices every day. **These daily choices will be your road map to get to your final dream destination.**

I want to encourage you to work through each phase until you feel that you have a solid plan that you can run with. Take your time developing each phase. The more you put into it, the more you will stay committed to it. You can take more or less time as you see fit, but I think a week is about right. A little time for seven days in a row, giving it time to soak in as you go along, and you'll never be the same. Enjoy the process!

YOUR BIG DREAM

"There is no grander sight in the world than that of a person filled with a great purpose, dominated by one unwavering aim."

—*Orison Swett Marden*

Everything in life is created twice. First something is created in the mind, in the form of a dream, vision, or idea. Then it is created a second time in reality, when strategy and planning are in place. Do you know why Dr. Martin Luther King Jr. wrote down and proclaimed his inspiring dream to all Americans? So he could create a dream in the hearts of every American. If he could rally a nation behind a dream, then everyone could move in the direction of creating it in reality. This is the point: *Everything starts with a dream.*

Trust me, people who don't have dreams become more and more careless about life. People with dreams have a reason to get up in the morning and work towards something bigger than themselves. Sometimes, the only dreams teens have for their campus are for themselves. They may just want to be popular, make decent grades, lay low and stay out of trouble, save up for a car, etc. If your dream is limited to selfish desires, then you won't make an impact on your classmates. You will go to school as a consumer, taking from the institution and not giving back. *My hope is that you would really dream big, and imagine in your mind's eye how awesome it would be to spark a movement of kindness among your peers.* Don't you want to leave high school knowing that you made it a better place for the upcoming generation?

You must have a BIG DREAM that gives you a sense of excitement, something that can rally your friends together. Besides, if you don't decide where your school is going, someone else will decide for you. This is what rips off most schools. Students don't take ownership of their school because they only care about having fun, instead of making a lasting impact. Not a good thing.

Having fun is fine, and in fact, it is crucial that you have fun in high school. BUT SCHOOL IS NO FUN WITH BULLIES AND HALLWAYS FILLED WITH HATE SPEECH!!! (Sorry for yelling.)

So, what is your dream? What is your unwavering aim? What is your great purpose? Don't even for a second think that you are too young or insignificant to come up with a vision for your school or your life. That is a lie. If you are capable of making choices that destroy your school (which you are) then you are capable of making choices that will build up your school. So let me ask you again. What is your vision for school? What is your big dream for life? If you don't know right now, don't stress. That's why I'm here. I've got the mad skills to draw this info out of you. Stand up for 10 seconds, stretch your pinky toes, and get a pen... 'cause when you sit back down I am going to evoke (google it) your Big Dream out of you.

You HAVE A DREAM

What would you like to see on your campus? Would you like to see hate erased from the hallways? Would you like to see separated cliques integrate more with each other? Do you want to see an explosion of acts of kindness and compassion? *Think about it, and write it down.* There is something amazingly powerful about getting this down in black and white. It sort of makes it official. It gets the dream out of your head and into the physical world for the first time.

This was my personal dream for my school:

I have a dream that, one day, the bully in all of us will cease to exist and that the words spoken in this school will build us up and not tear us down.

I have a dream that students in need will get support from their peers and that kids struggling with math or science, speech or biology, wouldn't have to seek out a teacher for help, but seek out a friend.

I have a dream that the kids in special education, who suffer from a multitude of disabilities, will be the true heroes of our school, and that they will feel loved, supported, and included in all of our activities.

I have a dream that our sports teams and all competitive clubs will set a standard of excellence so that our school's reputation would be legend among our community.

I have a dream that all prejudices, differences, or offenses will be swallowed up in our love for each other, and our commitment to our tolerance.

Now it's your turn: *I have a dream...*

Extra Credit!

Okay, sweet! You got your dream out of you! That's amazing. Way too many people never do what you just did... they just wander through life going with the flow. Not you. You've just taken the first step to direct your life and make it count. Now, if you are up for it, I want you to share it with me and the world! Tape yourself reading your I Have a Dream speech. Post it on youtube and send me the link: [brooks@brooksgibbs.com]. I will probably post it on my website and you will become world famous!

Now get some rest. Tomorrow we take the next step.

THE FUTURE YOU

"The highest expression of destiny awareness is a personal mission statement that captures the essence of your life purpose as you currently understand it."

—Steve Moore

This next truth is freakin' brilliant, if I may say so myself... which I just did. **If you want to be the person of your dreams, you must begin with the end in mind.** The way you are going to personally live out your dream is by writing a personal mission statement. This one-sentence mission statement is what you will memorize and recite daily. Don't blow me off here. The greatest leaders in the world attribute much of their success to having a clear mental image of where they want to go and who they want to be. Every great leader I have ever read about had some sort of life mission statement. I know that the word "personal mission statement" is quite intimidating. Don't freak out. It's easy to do, yet it will make a monster difference in the course of your life. For starters, I just want you to think about your life up until graduation. If you think about the near future, and the goals and dreams you have, it will be easier to write this important statement.

Here is the main reason I want you to get a vision for your life and school. **If you aim at nothing, you will hit it every time.** You have to aim for something that inspires you to become a better person. Living a successful and healthy life does not happen without intentional strategy. It takes a clear written plan of action and a daily re-commitment to see it through.

Because choosing to make right choices will sometimes be incredibly difficult, you will sometimes have to go against the crowd. There is no guarantee that bullies will stop doing their thing even if you do what's right. They have to choose for themselves to live above the line, but we can show the way and reap the benefits even if they stay in bondage to bullying.

Having a strong dream and personal mission statement for your life and school provides the strongest motivation I can think of to fuel your courage. You have to be willing to stand up and make the right decision despite any opposition that you have. **Noble dreams demand that you live like no one else—so that one day you can live like no one else.** Think about that. If you are willing to commit to your dream, your friends may laugh at your laser-beam focus now. But in the end, they will all be inspired by your commitment and example. That's the straight up truth. You will forever be remembered as the person who made others better, by your life's example!

I suggest that you follow this template:

Right now, my personal mission is to _____

(two or three action verbs), _____

(for/with/to whom statement) in order to _____

_____

_____ *(two or three worthy causes).*

Here, I will give you mine as an example:

My name is Brooks Gibbs.

Right now, my personal mission is to inspire and equip (action verbs) those around me, especially my peers, (for/with/to whom statement) in order to show extreme kindness to others, to make a positive impact in their community, and to walk in Truth and Wisdom every day of their life (two or three worthy causes).

Some other teens purpose statements:

My name is Billy Armstrong.

Right now, my personal mission is to direct and collaborate (action verbs) with other students, (for/with/to whom) events that bring our school together and service projects that reach our community (worthy causes).

My name is Erica Murphy.

Right now, my personal mission is to connect and encourage (action verbs) fellow students, (for/with/to whom) to thrive in friendship, experience peer to peer support, and achieve academic success through study groups (worthy causes).

My name is Brian Nicholas.

Right now, my personal mission is to grow, mature, and develop (action verbs) my character, talents, and faith, (for/with/to whom) so that I can maintain a respectable reputation, achieve academic and athletic success, and be an example to my peers (worthy causes).

Got the idea? Yeah, it's not tough; it just has to be *you*! Don't just borrow your dream from someone else; think it through and make it yours. So go ahead, and take some time to work on your life purpose statement right now. Chances are that you are going to tweak it quite a bit as time goes on. But you have to start somewhere. So take a stab at it right now. Do it. I'm watching you... like Santa.

My name is _____

Right now, my life purpose is to _____
(action verbs) _____
(for/with/to whom statement) in order to _____

_____

_____

_____

_____ *(two or three worthy causes).*

If you do what I am asking you to do, you will be one in a million. Most people don't take their life this seriously, and you can tell. But, if you choose to value your life and your future this much, you will be willing to define yourself and create a personal mission statement—and you will stand out in the crowd. You will be committed to march to the beat of your own drum. You will be going against the stream of mediocrity. While other teens settle for an immature and lame life, you will be striving for something much more meaningful. I don't know about you, but I am tired of people viewing teens as brainless juveniles without direction. Let's debunk these low expectations! Go for it! Stay committed, be an example to those watching you, and inspire them to follow in your footsteps.

Then go reward yourself with a Red Bull Float or something. Whatever you consume, just make sure it has loads of sugar in it, because you're going to need the buzz for tomorrow's assignment!

DAY 3

YOUR CORE VALUES

"You must grow to realize your dreams. Your dream will appear on the horizon, not at arm's length. It is up to you to create the path that will reach it."
—*Steve Moore*

Okay, you rock. Day 3 and you're still going strong. Good thing. Now, I'm about to dig even deeper. I am about to probe around in your heart like no one ever has. But I am so excited, because you are about to define your values. When you do this your life will NEVER be the same. Game on. If you are going to see your big dream come true, and live your personal mission statement to the max, than you need to develop a few core values to help you get there. Core values are words that describe your character. (Example: Compassion, Kindness, Empathy, etc.) They are principles that you are striving to live by. They should be the driving force of your life. **I believe what you cherish at your core is what you aim at with your life.** Deciding on your core values is an exciting process, because once you articulate what the top three are, you will re-organize your whole life around them. They are that powerful! In my opinion, they are the secret motivation you will need to see your dream come true and live out your personal mission statement.

BEN FRANKLIN'S CORE VALUES

One of the most inspirational men I have ever studied was from Philadelphia. You probably know him as one of the Fathers of the United States, a great leader and diplomat. He signed the major documents of the founding of the U.S., including the Declaration of Independence and the Constitution. Maybe you know him as an inventor, or as a brilliant scientist who flew kites in lightning storms (so maybe he wasn't *all* brilliant), or as a writer and printing press operator. But did you know that in 1726, at the age of 20, while on an 80-day ocean voyage from London back to Philadelphia, Benjamin Franklin developed a "Plan" for reaching his future dreams?

He followed the plan he created "pretty faithfully" even to the age of 79 (when he wrote about it), and he was even more determined to stick with it for his remaining days because of the happiness he had enjoyed so far by following it.

His "Plan" was made up of 13 virtues (values), each with short descriptions:

1. **Temperance:** Eat not to dullness and drink not to elevation.

2. **Silence:** Speak not but what may benefit others or yourself. Avoid trifling conversation.

3. **Order:** Let all your things have their places. Let each part of your business have its time.

4. **Resolution:** Resolve to perform what you ought. Perform without fail what you resolve.

5. **Frugality:** Make no expense but to do good to others or yourself: i.e., waste nothing.

6. **Industry:** Lose no time. Be always employed in something useful. Cut off all unnecessary actions.

7. **Sincerity:** Use no hurtful deceit. Think innocently and justly; and, if you speak, speak accordingly.

8. **Justice:** Wrong none, by doing injuries or omitting the benefits that are your duty.

9. **Moderation:** Avoid extremes. Forebear resenting injuries so much as you think they deserve.

10. **Cleanliness:** Tolerate no uncleanness in body, clothes or habitation.

11. **Chastity:** Rarely use venery but for health or offspring; Never to dullness, weakness, or the injury of your own or another's peace or reputation.

12. **Tranquility:** Be not disturbed at trifles, or at accidents common or unavoidable.

13. **Humility:** Imitate Jesus and Socrates.

He committed to giving strict attention to one virtue each week so after 13 weeks he moved through all 13. After 13 weeks he would start the process over again so in one year he would complete the course a total of four times. He tracked his progress by using a little book of 13 charts. At the top of each chart was one of the virtues. The charts had a column for each day of the week and thirteen rows marked with the first letter of each of the 13 virtues. Every evening he would review the day and put a mark (dot) next to each virtue for each fault committed with respect to that virtue for that day.

FORM OF THE PAGES.

TEMPERANCE.

Eat not to dulness; drink not to elevation.

	Sun.	M.	T.	W.	Th.	F.	S.
Tem.							
Sil.	*	*		*		*	
Ord.	*	*			*	*	*
Res.		*				*	
Fru.		*				*	
Ind.			*				
Sinc.							
Jus.							
Mod.							
Clea.							
Trans.							
Chas.							
Hum.							

Naturally, his goal was to live his days and weeks without having to put any marks on his chart. Initially he found himself putting more marks on these pages than he ever imagined, but in time he enjoyed seeing them diminish. After a while he went through the series only once per year and then only once in several years until finally omitting them entirely. But he always carried the little book with him as a reminder. Benjamin Franklin's 13 virtues are unique and obviously served him well since he is one of the most respected and most accomplished men in the history of the United States.

He wasn't great by chance, but because he chose a plan.

PURSUING YOUR CORE VALUES WITH PASSION

The importance of pursuing your core values with absolute passion can be illustrated by this story:

Once upon a time, there was a man whose job was to find pearls, buy them, and then re-sell them for a profit. One day he was going about his business as usual when a pearl diver pulled him aside and whispered, "I have the most exquisite pearl in the world." The merchant chuckled and thought, That's what they all say. To the diver he said, "Okay, son, let's see what you have." The diver glanced around, then pulled the merchant further into the shadows of a nearby building. Slowly, he pulled out a small bundle. He opened fold after fold of cloth, until shimmering before the merchant was, indeed, the most exquisite pearl in the world! He gasped. Suddenly nothing else he owned mattered compared to that glowing white sphere. "Don't show that to anyone. I'll be back in three days, ready to pay whatever you ask."

The merchant quickly liquidated everything he owned. He sold his house, his furnishings, his flocks and herds, his baseball card collection, and all the rest of his pearls. Then, at great cost, he returned and took ownership of one pearl. Just one. But he valued that pearl above all else. And with his purchase, he had gained his heart's greatest desire.[6]

When you discover your core values, that's exactly how you will respond. Your core values will rearrange and direct your energies, your time, and your thoughts. Once you identify your three core values, you will keep them close to you, hoping that you will get closer to them. As you identify and pursue them, you'll unleash your potential and set yourself up for fulfillment and success.

So let me ask you, what core values will you need to accomplish your dream?

If you want to launch service projects in your school, than SERVICE would be a great core value of yours. Or if you want to make sure students' needs are met, than COMPASSION is a great core value to choose. Don't think about what your friends value, what your school or community values, or even your family. I want you to think about what YOU value. Go ahead and look through this list of values and circle your top three. If you don't see a word that you want, just add it to the list. This is just here to help spark your thinking. (It may help you to pick your top 20, and then narrow it down to 15, 10, 5, and then 3. That's what helped me.)

Adventure, Attitude, Authenticity, Autonomy, Boldness, Challenges, Change, Character, Collaboration, Community, Compassion, Competence, Competition, Confidence, Cooperation, Courage, Creativity, Dedication, Devotion, Decisiveness, Discipline, Discovery, Diversity, Ecology/ environment, Education, Efficiency, Encouragement, Endurance, Enthusiasm, Ethics, Excellence, Excitement, Fairness, Faith, Faithfulness, Fame, Family, Flexibility, Freedom, Friendship, Generosity, Gentleness, Goodness, Gratefulness, Growth, Happiness, Health, Helping Others, Honesty, Honor, Hope, Humility, Humor, Independence, Integrity, Intimacy, Joy, Justice, Kindness, Leadership, Learning, Love, Loyalty, Meaningful Work, Mercy, Money, Obedience, Openness, Order, Passion, Patience, Peace, Perseverance, Personal Growth, Philanthropy, Play, Power, Prayer, Privacy, Purity, Recognition, Relationships, Reliability, Religion, Respect, Sacrifice, Safety, Security, Self-control, Self-discipline, Selfless, Service, Spirituality, Stability, Steadfast, Teachable, Teamwork, Thankfulness, Tolerance, Transparency, Trustworthiness, Truth, Unity, Wealth, Wisdom, Work.

Now write your core values below.

1. _____

2. _____

3. _____

Now, write them one more time, but this time write a very brief description of what that value means to you, just like Ben Franklin did...but you can skip the weird old language, okay? None of the "Rarely use venery but for health or offspring" stuff. Use your own words.

1. _____

_____

_____

_____

2. _____

_____

_____

_____

3. _____

_____

_____

_____

Got it? Are you still with me? I hope so, because this is mammoth. Listen, most people never, ever get around to doing this. But you just did. You took a moment to define what the rest of your life (at least your time in high school) will look like.

Now I want you to take a bit of a risk. I want you to share this with a friend you trust. Call them up and share what's been happening these last couple of days. If you don't have a friend you trust, call your great-aunt Gertrude. She will say, "That's real sweet, Dear. Now how come you never come visit me?" When she does that, just politely ask for more money.

AFFIRMATION STATEMENTS

You now know, in your head, what your core values are—simply powerful! Today we're going to get it from your head into your heart so that it can be released in your life. We're going to do that with an "affirmation statement." Don't freak out, these are simple and easy. I guarantee this is about a billion times easier than forgiving someone. If you can do that, I know you can do this! Now that you have picked your top 3 values, I want you to write an affirmation statement under each value. It is written in the affirmative, meaning that you are already living it out. And it's also written using "I" language, meaning that it's about you, because change begins with who? Yeah that's right, you.

Let me give you a couple of examples:

CoRE VALUE:
Selfless

Affirmation Statement: I am continually putting the needs of others before my own, so that I might be helpful to others and show them genuine love.

CoRE VALUE:
Kindness

Affirmation Statement: I take great care to respond kindly to others by my words and actions.

CoRE VALUE:
Encouragement

Affirmation Statement: I have the ability to lift a sorrowful person up high by my encouraging words.

Alright…it's your turn. Go ahead and write an affirmation statement for each of your new core values!

CoRE VALUE: _____
Affirmation Statement:

_____

_____

_____

_____

CoRE VALUE: _____
Affirmation Statement:

_____

_____

_____

_____

CoRE VALUE: _____
Affirmation Statement:

_____

_____

_____

_____

Now, I double-dog-dare you to start reading those values every day. Put them by your bed and read them out loud as the first thing you do when you get up, and the last thing you do before you hit the sack.

Core values are simply those virtues which you must have in your life to make yourself the best you can be. Whatever word you picked as your core value—you need to study it like crazy! Google your core values and see what pops up. You must get to know the meaning of that core value better than any other word.

At one point, *self-discipline* was one of my core values. So, I went to work and read as many books as I could about the subject. I also practiced different ways to exercise my self-discipline, like fasting from food for 3 or 4 days, interviewing people in my life who I thought showed incredible self-discipline, and reading biographies of people who exemplified this characteristic.

Writing your core values along with an affirmation statement is a fantastic start. Take it to the next step and find ways to learn more about that value until you are able to live and breathe that core value without even thinking! (Yeah, I am hardcore, and you should be too.)

Try me on this, okay? I want you to give it a shot. Put those affirmation statements by your bed, or even in the bathroom where I *know* you'll have a minute or two everyday to sit and think about them. (Did I go too far?) Might as well use the time for something that will transform your life. Anyway, I'm just saying that if you take these core values and affirmation statements to heart, it's going to be amazing.

After a month, email me at brooks@brooksgibbs.com and tell me what's happening!

EXTRA CREDIT!

It is really good to envision what your day would look like if you lived out these core values. A good way to envision these values in action is to do a short writing exercise. Write out what your perfect day looks like, from the moment you awaken to when your head hits the pillow at night. Describe your surroundings, whom you are with, and how you lived out your core values. Just walk through your most ideal day. Don't hold back or limit yourself. This day belongs to you and no one else. This may be pretend, but it will help you envision yourself actually living out your core values and fulfilling your personal mission statement.

Dear Diary,

Today was a great day...

YOUR DAILY CHOICES

"Goals are dreams with deadlines."

—Diana Scharf Hunt

So you have your dream, your mission statement, your core values, and now you have affirmation statements too. Cool. Now, imagine you are about to take a road trip somewhere super exciting! You can't wait to get there. The destination represents your *big dream*. You need gas right? Of course, without gas you would only make it a fraction of the distance and your engine would just stall out. The gas in the car represents your *core values*, the characteristics that you know you need to see your dream come true. Finally, to get to your dream you will need a road map. You can't just wish yourself there. You can't just drive aimlessly. You need step by step directions, and this map represents your *daily choices.*

We only have 24 hours in a day, and what we decide to do with that time will determine what we accomplish. If we choose to be lazy that day, we won't accomplish anything, and therefore we will never make progress with anything. That is not the way I want to live. The choices you make every day will determine whether or not you will see your dream come to reality. So that is why you must keep your dream, mission statement, and core values close to you every day. You don't want to get lazy or give up the dream, right?

You need a daily plan to live these things out. You need to daily incorporate these things in your every day life. Because I have realized that **life is made up of a series of choices; and choices have consequences.** You and I have dozens of major decisions we make each day. When we write out our goals, we are planning out our dreams on paper. Each step in achieving a goal is a step toward making a dream come true. This is where the rubber meets the road. You should write specific goals and ask yourself every day, "What can I choose to do today to get closer to completing my goals?" I want you to think about what goals you need to set in order to see your big dream come true. Write down goals that would help you get closer to your dream, and make sure you write action steps for each goal and always give them a deadline.

Example:

Daniel, from San Antonio, Texas has a dream to see bullying end on his campus. So here are some of his specific goals and action steps for this year:

GoAL:

Do a school-wide survey to assess the "bullying temperature" of our school.

Deadline: *September 15*

Action Step 1: Write questions that will be on the survey.

Action Step 2: Have a few people critique them to make them better.

Action Step 3: Get permission from the administration to pass out surveys.

Action Step 4: Print out 500 copies of the survey.

Action Step 5: Make announcements the morning of, and pass out the surveys during lunch.

GOAL:

Create and run a poster campaign on campus to promote kind words.

Deadline: *October 1*

Action Step 1: Brainstorm what the posters should look like based on the feedback received from the surveys.

Action Step 2: Get a graphic artist to do a mock-up of the posters.

Action Step 3: Get a few friends to vote on the best posters.

Action Step 4: Print posters, and get permission to post them around campus.

GOAL:

Organize a pro-kindness assembly for the whole school to attend.

Deadline: *November 15*

Action Step 1: Get information about Brooks Gibbs' assembly program.

Action Step 2: Get permission from the administration to do it.

Action Step 3: Book Brooks Gibbs to come speak at our school.

Action Step 4: Promote it around school to create an exciting buzz.

GOAL:

Launch a "kindness committee" to pioneer more ways to end bullying.

Deadline: *November 23*

Action Step 1: Make an announcement at the assembly that we are starting one.

Action Step 2: Hold a meeting to see who wants to join.

Action Step 3: Create job descriptions for each member.

Action Step 4: Create the committee's big corporate dream with goals and action steps.

Your turn! Take a quick look back at your mission statement, core values and affirmation statements. Give it a little thought and then write some goals and action steps for this year:

GOAL: _____

    Deadline: _____

    Action Step 1: _____

    Action Step 2: _____

    Action Step 3: _____

    Action Step 4: _____

GOAL: _____

    Deadline: _____

    Action Step 1: _____

    Action Step 2: _____

    Action Step 3: _____

    Action Step 4: _____

GOAL: _____

    Deadline: _____

    Action Step 1: _____

    Action Step 2: _____

    Action Step 3: _____

    Action Step 4: _____

Goals and Action Steps are constantly changing. Plans change. Circumstances change. So be ready to *always flex your goals with the changes that are taking place around you.* I like to print these things out on paper and then post them around my house. I also transfer them onto my phone so that I can review them every day, no matter where I am. Why am I so obsessed about keeping this stuff so close to me? Because life is a lot like a football game. You can have great training, a great team, and a great coach—but unless you are strategically trying to reach the goal line, and unless you know what plays you need to get there, it's going to be a losing season... and it would really stink to lose in life simply because you didn't have a plan.

So way to go! Now you have the goals and the action steps to make dreams become reality.

ACCOUNTABILITY NETWORK

Unless you are a highly motivated and focused person, just having goals and action steps won't be enough to succeed. You need a network of people to hold you accountable to get these things done! In my personal experience, when I have an accountability network, I am 10 times more likely to meet my deadlines and reach my goals and action steps. This concept may be unfamiliar to you, but believe me, it works.

Your accountability network is made up of people that you choose to keep you accountable to your goals, and they will contact you on a specified date to see if you need help, making sure that you meet your deadlines. This really provides the motivation you need for success. There is nothing like a person you trust kicking you in the pants every once in a while to get things done. (Not in a mean, bully-like way of course!)

Your accountability network will be made up of two types of people: Friends and Grown-ups.

Friends: Friends are great sources of accountability. They look UP at you, depending on you to lead them. You should share with them your goals and encourage them to keep you accountable to the deadline. They may even want to join you, helping you out with practical needs. Definitely take them up on it. Also, they may be so inspired by your goals that they want to write up their own. Be sure to help them do this. The more people working towards a dream, the better!

Grown-Ups: You really should get a couple of adults as your main source of accountability. They are looking DOWN at you—in a good way—ready to give you a hand up to the next level. I know, I know, adults aren't always "cool," but they are wise, and probably way more responsible than your friends, and they will most likely follow through with keeping you accountable. Usually, every school has one or two people on staff that would make great accountability partners. Ask them. They will be all over it!

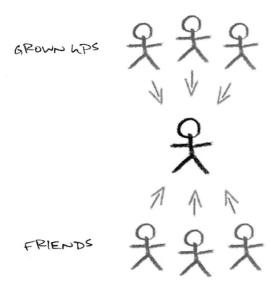

THREE WORDS OF WISDOM

1. You need an accountability <u>network</u> and not just one accountability partner. No matter how much your friends or grown-ups love and care about you, they are bound to forget every once in a while that you need to be kicked in the pants to meet your deadlines. That is why I suggest that you have a minimum of three people to hold you accountable on each goal. This way, if one of them flakes on you, at least you have another person to step up and hold you accountable.

2. You need to update them monthly. Send them a monthly update that tells them what is going on in your life, what you need advice on, and how you are progressing towards your goals. My suggestion is to send them this update via email on the first Monday of every month. This is powerful, because it will help them stay connected with you and know exactly what is going on.

3. Your accountability needs to be <u>formal</u>. You can't just ask someone, "Hey, can you call me every once in a while to make sure I get this thing done?" Chances are, the person will gladly offer to hold you accountable, but then forget to contact you. That is why when you invite someone to be a part of your accountability network, you should formally lay out your expectation. Give them a print out of your goals, action steps, and deadlines. Then ask them to contact you one week before each deadline. If you really want them to hold you accountable, I suggest making it as easy as possible for them by telling them exactly what date to contact you, and exactly what you want them to ask you.

Example:

Dear Jake, thanks so much for being part of my accountability network. Your relationship is absolutely key to successfully completing my goals. I want to make this really easy for you, so I will lay out exactly what I expect from you.

Please call me on September 20th and ask me these questions: "Did you finish making the posters? Did you get permission to do the assembly? Is there anything that is holding you back from accomplishing your goal next week?"

Please call me on October 15th and ask me, "Did you get permission from the administration to hold an assembly, and did you put together a proposed budget for the big event?"

Make a list of people who you can recruit to be a part of your accountability network, and then contact them to formally invite them to help make your dream come true!

Friends:

_____

_____

_____

_____

Grown-Ups:

_____

_____

_____

_____

Congratulations! You have successfully completed a very, very powerful planning process! If you have come this far into the book, you have proved that you are a mature individual who really cares about making a positive difference in your school and—perhaps even more important than that—you have proven that you have the values and the character to change your life for the rest of your life and maybe even bring others along with you!

Now go for it and never look back!

MAKE IT REAL

Wow, just a few pages left to go! There is one last thing I want you to do before we say our goodbyes: Compile all of the stuff you just wrote onto one sheet that will be easy to post in your room, car, and locker. Put it on paper. **Make it real.** *Make it tangible.* Post it and make it that much easier to remember. The one sheet should look something like this:

NAME: DANIEL MORELAND

BIG DREAM:

I have a dream that bullying will end on our campus, and all students will choose kind words over hate speech.

PERSONAL MISSION STATEMENT:

My mission is to pave the way and lead the students of my school, in the direction of kindness, compassion, and tolerance.

CORE VALUES:

Kindness. My words and actions are consistently positive and uplifting.

Leadership. I am paving the way for my school to change for the better.

Organization. I am becoming better organized so that I can lead more efficiently and move more quickly towards my dreams.

GOAL:

Do a school-wide survey to assess the "bullying temperature" of our school.

Deadline: *September 15*

Action Steps: Write questions that will be on the survey.

Action Steps: Have a few people critique them, to make them better.

Action Steps: Print out 500 copies of the survey.

Action Steps: Get permission from the administration to pass out surveys.

Action Steps: Make announcements the morning of, and pass out the surveys during lunch.

GOAL:

Create and run a poster campaign on campus to promote kind words.

Deadline: October 1

Action Steps: Brainstorm what the posters should look like based on the feedback received from the surveys.

Action Steps: Get a graphic artist to do a mock-up of the posters.

Action Steps: Get a few friends to vote on the best posters.

Action Steps: Print posters, and get permission to post them around campus.

ACCOUNTABILITY NETWORK:

Friends: Brian, James, Bianca, and Josh.

Grown-ups: Steve, Joan, Reba, Chris, and Jeff.

If you've been working on a computer, it should just require you to cut and paste to get this together. Afterwards, updating it as you grow and change will really be a piece of cake. Please do this. It will only take a few minutes. When you are done, hold it up and take a look. What you hold in your hand isn't just a piece of paper with some words. Instead, it's a powerful document, a plan to make your dreams come true, because it's true about you.

SEIZING THE DREAM

In 1963, Dr. Martin Luther King Jr. gave his famous "I Have A Dream" speech. These famous words still inspire us today. Read them again, and let them add fuel to the fire of your dream:

I have a dream that one day this nation will rise up and live out the true meaning of its creed: "We hold these truths to be self-evident: that all men are created equal."

I have a dream that one day on the red hills of Georgia the sons of former slaves and the sons of former slave owners will be able to sit down together at the table of brotherhood...

I have a dream that my four little children will one day live in a nation where they will not be judged by the color of their skin but by the content of their character.

I have a dream today...

When we allow freedom to ring, when we let it ring from every village and every hamlet, from every state and every city, we will be able to speed up that day when all of God's children, black men and white men, Jews and Gentiles, Protestants and Catholics, will be able to join hands and sing in the words of the old Negro spiritual, "Free at last! Free at last! Thank God Almighty, we are free at last!"

This inspiring dream is closer to becoming reality now more than ever before in the history of our country. It is awesome to see how far we have come, yet it is humbling to see how far we still have to go. It is a testament to our ability to climb the moral mountain of justice. It may not be easy for Americans to change how we treat one another, but we have proven that it is totally possible! This encourages me that your generation has a chance to make even more progress.

Back in the introduction, I said, "Welcome to the World of Bullies. Bullies are everywhere. Just look around your school and you will see bullying all around you, and not just the typical big-guy-beating-up-the-little-guy routine. Bullying is much broader than that stereotype."

Now I say, "Welcome to the World of Life-changers. Life-changers are everywhere. Just look around your school and you'll see people who are able and willing to make tremendous changes on your campus. Not just the student council presidents or the captain of the basketball team... no, life-changers are much broader than that stereotype."

Change, as you now know, begins with you. Love is the key, because it is greater than hate. One person making a call to change in the name of love can be the spark that creates a movement that multiplies and spreads throughout an entire school and community. Is it too much to dream of a team of life-changers from every corner of your campus coming together? What if a group of life-changers— from the freaks and the geeks, the jocks and the band nerds, the drama queens and the dance squad—what if, just what if you all came together in the same room determined to make a difference?

Most teens don't realize that the spirit of their school is completely influenced by them. You are the one who can most powerfully change the culture in your school. It only takes one person with a dream and a plan. I hope that this book has given you everything you need to start a movement towards kindness. That is the best way I believe that we can silence the bully.

You can join the growing movement of young people who are taking matters into their own hands by starting a domino effect of love—changing every student in the school for the better.

You really can. Trust me. I've been there, on both sides.

That's my dream. What's yours?

BROOKS GIBBS

P.S. It would be an honor to hear from you. I would love for you to send me a copy of your one-sheet that contains your mission, values and goals.

If you have any other questions, please don't hesitate to hit me up—I can be reached by e-mail at brooks@brooksgibbs.com. Also, check out my website for the latest info at www.BrooksGibbs.com.

END NOTES

1. 2010 PACER Center, Inc.

2. Advice from Josh Shipp, adapted from his program: "Hey Josh, How do I deal with being labeled?" Used with permission.

3. Source: advancementproject.org.

4. Mahatma Gandhi was an Indian Philosopher, internationally esteemed for his doctrine of nonviolent protest, 1869-1948.

5. The Pais Project is an organization made up of young people who have graduated high school and commit to give a year of their life to mentoring students. These heroic young adults are doing work all around the globe reaching hundreds of thousands of students each year. While most college age students are obsessed with themselves (thinking: where they will go to college, who they will hang out with, what they will wear...), these students are going beyond the call of duty and selflessly pouring into students in a positive way.

6. Creative illustration of biblical parable based on Craig Groeschel's book, *Chazown*, pg. 38.

WORK IT OUT

LIFE PURPOSE:

My name is _____

Right now, my life purpose is to _____

(action verbs) _____

(for/with/to whom statement) in order to _____

_____

_____

_____

_____

_____ *(two or three worthy causes).*

WORK IT OUT

LIFE PURPOSE:

My name is _____

Right now, my life purpose is to _____
(action verbs) _____
(for/with/to whom statement) in order to _____

_____

_____

_____

_____

_____ *(two or three worthy causes).*

WORK IT OUT

CoRE VALuE:

Affirmation Statement:

CoRE VALuE:

Affirmation Statement:

CoRE VALuE:

Affirmation Statement:

WORK IT OUT

CORE VALUE:

Affirmation Statement:

CORE VALUE:

Affirmation Statement:

CORE VALUE:

Affirmation Statement:

WORK IT OUT

CORE VALUE:

Affirmation Statement:

CORE VALUE:

Affirmation Statement:

CORE VALUE:

Affirmation Statement:

WORK IT OUT

BIG DREAM: What would you like to see changed?

GOAL:

    Deadline:

    Action Step 1:

    Action Step 2:

    Action Step 3:

    Action Step 4:

GOAL:

    Deadline:

    Action Step 1:

    Action Step 2:

    Action Step 3:

    Action Step 4:

WORK IT OUT

BIG DREAM: What would you like to see changed?

GOAL:

    Deadline:

    Action Step 1:

    Action Step 2:

    Action Step 3:

    Action Step 4:

GOAL:

    Deadline:

    Action Step 1:

    Action Step 2:

    Action Step 3:

    Action Step 4:

NOTES

NOTES

CPSIA information can be obtained at www.ICGtesting.com
Printed in the USA
LVOW120937050212

267139LV00008B/94/P